# Praise for *Bu*

*How to Write a Book to Spotlight Your Expertise,*
*Attract a Ton of New Customers, and Explode Your Profits!*

"*Business Gold* is a practical and insightful handbook to get your ideas into writing and then get them published into a book that can clearly demonstrate your expertise. Now that I've read it, I want to go back and rewrite a couple of my previously published books! This book will take years off your learning curve and reduce your frustration with writing as well. If you ever want to write a book, this is your key to success."

—Michael Soon Lee, MBA
President, EthnoConnect
Author, *Cross-Cultural Selling for Dummies,*
*Black Belt Negotiating*, and many other books
www.EthnoConnect.com

"In today's hypercompetitive world, a prospect-targeted book that highlights one's expertise is a marketing must-have. To maximize your ROI, it needs to be done well, from beginning to end. That's where *Business Gold* becomes your best friend.

In a word, *Business Gold* is comprehensive. From developing your book concept to writing, illustrating, publishing, and marketing, if you need to know it, it's in here. This is the go-to source for any entrepreneur or business professional who not only needs to write a book, but needs to write one that highlights the author's business as a leading authority in its industry.

With this one book, Tammy Barley assists you to attract tons of new customers, recession-proof your business, and command higher fees, because your published book will broadcast you as an expert."

—Danita Bye
Founder and CEO, Sales Growth Specialists
*Named Power Player by* Minnesota Business *magazine in 2010*
www.SalesGrowthSpecialists.com

"Having written, edited, and published twenty-six books myself, I know firsthand the amount of time, effort, and expense involved in getting a book written, published, and into the marketplace. When I suffered a serious health challenge and learned that

I might only have a few months to live, I needed help in getting a message of hope and inspiration into the hands of others who were struggling with their own life and business challenges. I turned my project over to Tammy Barley, and in record time she had my audio transcripts edited, formatted, and turned into a finished project—in less than three weeks. Tammy is an expert at her craft, and her book, *Business Gold*, gives you the exact formula that she used.

If you have a book in your head and need to get it into printed form and into the eyes and minds of your business prospects or other people who can benefit from your message, don't waste any time—get this book, apply the step-by-step process she lays out, and get it into the marketplace. Tammy makes it so easy!"

—Martin Howey
CEO, TopLine Business Solutions
*Known worldwide as the number one resource*
*for training and supporting marketing and*
*business-development consultants*
www.TopLineBusinessSolutions.com

"At last! *THIS* is the book business authors have needed for years. If you're like me, you've had a book in your head for some time but never completed it because of the overwhelming questions about "How do I . . . ?" Now there is a solution—*Business Gold*. This easy-to-follow, informative, and entertaining book is one resource every self-publishing business author must have.

*Business Gold* takes you one easy step at a time through book-concept development, expression of your brand, and how to provide valuable content your prospective clients are eager for while distinguishing you from your competition. *Business Gold* also gives tons of ideas for custom graphics that will capture the attention of your readers and make your information stick, then teaches you how to self-publish, e-publish, and market your book. I can't think of a single question I might have had that the author, Tammy Barley, didn't answer, or of another source that better helps entrepreneurs to spotlight their expertise through the publication of their own book.

Tammy Barley enabled me to complete my first business book, and now her expertise is available to you too through *Business Gold!*"

—Mike Shannon, Author,
*Fortune 1000 Companies' sales-growth expert*
Founder and CEO, Axiom Development
www.AxiomDevelopment.com

# *Business Gold*

## How to Write a Book
## to Spotlight Your Expertise,
## Attract a Ton of New Customers,
## and Explode Your Profits!

By Tammy Barley

The Millionaire Entrepreneurs'
Book Consultant

**with a Foreword by Robert Skrob**

Business Book Productions

*Business Gold: How to Write a Book to Spotlight Your Expertise, Attract a Ton of New Customers, and Explode Your Profits!*
Published by Business Book Productions
123 South Eastwood Drive #232
Woodstock, IL 60098 USA

Printed in the United States of America

ISBN-13: 978-0-615-73779-9
ISBN-10: 061573779X

The author would like to thank the individuals who graciously welcomed and permitted usage of interviews: Ann McIndoo, Jim Saurbaugh, Jim Palmer, and Brian Feinblum.

Cover design by Jim Saurbaugh, JS Graphic Design.
Interior art by Reece Montgomery.

Library of Congress Control Number: 2013903835

All Scripture quotations, unless otherwise indicated, are taken from the *Holy Bible, New International Version®. NIV®.* Copyright © 1973, 1978, 1984 by International Bible Society. Used by permission of Zondervan. All rights reserved.

DISCLAIMER AND/OR LEGAL NOTICES
While the publisher and author have used their best efforts in preparing this book, they make no representations or warranties with respect to the accuracy or completeness of the contents of this book. The advice and strategies contained herein may not be suitable for your situation. You should consult a professional where appropriate. Neither the publisher nor the author shall be liable for any loss of profit or any other commercial damages, including but not limited to special, incidental, consequential, or other damages. The purchaser or reader of this publication assumes responsibility for the use of these materials and information. Adherence to all applicable laws and regulations, both advertising and all other aspects of doing business in the United States or any other jurisdiction, is the sole responsibility of the purchaser or reader.

www.BusinessGoldTheBook.com
www.BusinessBookProductions.com

# Contents

## Part 1

## Develop Your Concept

i

# Part 2
# Write the Manuscript

# Part 3
# Edit: Polish to a Golden Finish

# Part 4

# Creative Artistry

# to Attract a Ton of New Customers

## Chapter 16
### Book-Cover Artistry:
### Interview with Graphic Designer Jim Saurbaugh................**179**

# Part 5
# Traditional-, Self-, or E-Publish

## Chapter 17
### Publishing Options: Traditional Publishing Houses ......**199**

## Chapter 18
### Publishing Options: Self-Publishing Companies............**208**

## Chapter 19
### Publishing Options: E-Publishing ....................................**212**

## Chapter 20
### How to Format Your Manuscript for Traditional Publication ..........**216**

## Part 6

# Market Your Book
# to Explode Your Profits!

# Foreword

## The Complicated, Made Simple
## by Robert Skrob

I cried when I saw it. I was able to hide the tears, but there it was. Sitting right there on the shelf. On the self at the bookstore of airside B of the Hartsfield-Jackson Atlanta International Airport. I had finally made it! All the work writing, rewriting, editing, proofing, and marketing had paid off. My book had gone from idea to the shelf of the bookstore.

I had a couple boxes of copies of the book at my office, but there was something special about finding it at the bookstore at the Atlanta airport. I grabbed a pen out of my bag, picked up the book, autographed it, and put it back on the shelf. Whoever came by that bookstore and bought that book got an autographed copy!

Congratulations on making it this far. You are already in the top 5 percent of the population because you took action on your dream of writing a book. You have a terrific resource in your hands to help you achieve it. Be proud that you are already far more ambitious than the vast majority of the population who don't think it's possible for them to ever write a book.

Allow me to warn you though, of the people who make the decision to write a book, only about 20 percent ever finish. And that's exactly why the resource you are holding is so important.

There's never been a more complete and thorough road map to take you by the hand and lead you through the book writing, publishing, and marketing process. Before today, authors had to grope around in the dark trying to find their way through the labyrinth of book writing and publishing options out there. You get all the lessons learned, from a professional book editor, in one convenient volume.

The fact so few people ever succeed in writing a book is actually a good thing for you. It distinguishes you from your competitors. As an author you separate yourself from all of your competitors who do not have a book of their own. You are the person who wrote the book. You are forever distinguished from the masses who don't have the guts to begin a book nor have the fortitude to stick with it.

Do you want to know the real secret? Authoring a book really isn't as difficult as it seems.

My daughter is seventeen years old and driving a car today, but getting her to learn how to ride her bicycle without training wheels was a challenge. She wanted to learn so she kept trying, but she got really frustrated. We pushed her through the grass in the front yard as she learned so she'd land in the grass rather on the concrete driveway.

Today she can get on a bike and ride it without a thought. Our son took to it more easily. He had his share of falls, but it wasn't nearly as frustrating as it was for our daughter.

And that's the secret of authoring a book. The first one will be challenging. It'll take a lot of work. When you are done, you'll look back and say to yourself, "That was easy! I have a lot more ideas I want to turn into a book."

Today I've authored or coauthored five books. I've found my books in bookstores around the country. I had a customer send me a photo of a book I'd authored taken at the bookstore at Harvard Business School.

Just like learning to ride a bike, learning to write a book for the first time will feel strange. Allow Tammy Barley to guide you, like a loving parent, through the process, step by step. And, when you get frustrated and run into problems, try again.

It's worth it. Once you learn this process, you'll discover how easy it really is. And, you'll be an author! I can't wait to read your book.

—Robert Skrob, CPA
Author, *Official Get Rich Guide to Information Marketing*
www.InfoMarketingBook.com

# Acknowledgments

This book could not have been written without the assistance and inspiration of many fellow book-industry enthusiasts and entrepreneurs. My sincere appreciation to Ann McIndoo, Jim Saurbaugh, Jim Palmer, and Brian Feinblum for your generosity of time and expert knowledge in your book-related fields.

An additional hat tip to Jim Saurbaugh and to Reece Montgomery for their phenomenal cover design and interior artistry.

Robert Skrob—you are an inspiration. To many.

A special thank you to Jim Palmer, my business coach, mentor, fellow brainstormer, and bottomless font of knowledge.

As always, immeasurable love and gratitude to my parents extraordinaire, and to the kiddos, the greatest three blessings God has ever bestowed on a mom.

Thank you to God for all of the above, and for the countless other blessings poured down and prayers answered, even the ones I never thought to ask.

One additional thank you to God for my phenomenal clients. You folks, the entrepreneurs, are the ones who create jobs and enable others to achieve great personal and professional success. What an awesome gift you give.

# A Letter to the Reader

Congratulations on your book-to-be! A new book is an exciting and important addition to your business, one that underscores you as a top expert in your field, spotlights your business as *the* go-to resource in your industry, and enables you to command higher fees as a result.

By providing a book packed with information your readers want, in a way they find enjoyable to read, you will draw fresh prospects into your new-business funnel, and solidify your relationships with existing customers or clients through the addition of this valuable asset.

Today, producing a book can deliver a higher ROI than ever before, and is easier than ever to produce. By using this means to position yourself as a leading expert and to command higher fees, it will help you to recession-proof your business, and provide the Information-Age solutions that are increasingly in demand.

What's more, readers impressed by your book will promote it to their associates as a must-read, and bring new business right to your doorstep, people eager to invest in the solutions your business provides.

All that remains is to write a book that impresses. That dazzles. That gets recommended as a must-read. The book you see before you is the vehicle that will enable you to make it happen.

My writing and editing career began in 2001. Since then, business professionals new to writing book-length manuscripts have asked me countless questions about the book-production process. To answer them all, even some you might not think to ask, I wrote *Business Gold:*

*How to Write a Book to Spotlight Your Expertise, Attract a Ton of New Customers, and Explode Your Profits!*

In the following pages you will find virtually everything you need to know to write, publish, and market your book, including interviews with four book-production industry gurus and URLs to people who can assist you and save you time.

You might be wondering why I include actual interviews rather than paraphrase experts' insight. For this book, paraphrasing was simply not good enough. To gain the most from this dream team, you need to hear their insights straight from them.

My goal is to provide you with everything you need to strike business gold with your book, step by step, simply presented, all in one place.

How do you use this book? Develop and write your book while you're reading this one, and when you turn the last page you'll be placing a book into readers' hands, one that will Spotlight Your Expertise, Attract a Ton of New Customers, and Explode Your Profits!

A quick side note. Naturally, I wrote this book for both men and women readers. Throughout the book, to avoid wordiness, I use "he," "him," and "his" rather than "he/she," "him/her," "his/hers." If your book's target readers are primarily women, by all means, use "she," "her," and "hers" in your book.

So here we are at the end of my introduction, and the start of your new book's success.

Wishing you business gold!

*Tammy Barley*

The Millionaire Entrepreneurs' Book Consultant

# Part 1

# Develop Your Concept

# An Important Note

---

# "Do I have a viable book concept?"

---

The first question many entrepreneurs ask me is, "Do I have a viable book concept?" My answer is this. If you have information to share that has not been published before (or has not been published in a unique way), if that information has an audience, and if that audience is large enough, and your goals important enough, to be worth the investment of your time and resources, then yes, you do have a viable concept.

Keep in mind that a business book is a tool. It's bait on your marketing hook, which you can use to entice new prospects into your business. Juicy bait, absolutely, but remember that a book isn't the proverbial hook, line, and sinker that will land your prospect; your business must provide those. A book also isn't a flick of the wrist away from landing on the best-seller shelf. Neither is it going to generate a boatload of income from copies sold. It is bait.

Juicy bait.

Use your book to position yourself as a leading expert in your field and to underscore your expertise. Use it to draw prospects into your funnel.

"How exactly does it draw in new prospects?" you wonder? Because it allows prospects to get to know, like, and trust you, to make a small purchase, and with it sample what it means to work with you, and with your business. They become comfortable, even excited, with the small investment of the book and the great content and solutions it delivers, leading them to be comfortable going to you for a more substantial purchase.

Your goal for producing a book shouldn't be wealth from copies sold, but to create the ultimate tool. The most enticing bait.

Book sales won't make you money. You'll make money because the book sells you.

With that goal in mind, I will now show you what it takes to ensure your book's success.

# Chapter 1

# The Two Keys
# to a Book's Success

A book's success depends on two key factors:

1. Selling the book to potential readers
2. Inspiring those purchasers to network subsequent sales for you via enthusiastic word-of-mouth referrals—which is, and always will be, the best way to sell subsequent copies

Each of those may sound simple enough, but each involves a number of steps to achieve and several elements you need to consider and develop as you produce your book. I'll detail those steps and elements for you, one by one.

Let's look at the first factor—selling the book to potential readers.

To sell your book, it must grab potential readers visually and intellectually. That means your book needs compelling images and great content that your business prospects want and that none of your competitors provides.

Think about a book sale from the viewpoint of a potential buyer. When you stand in a store and consider whether to purchase a book, what parts of a book do you evaluate? If you're like most potential buyers, you scan the row of spines on each shelf and read the titles. If a title seems promising, you slide the book out and eye its cover.

Either the cover art grabs you, or it doesn't. Still gazing at the front cover, you skim the book's subtitle or description, and the one-line testimonial that concisely describes and praises the book, and often suggests its target audience. You notice the name of the person who supplied that quote, a highly respected professional well known to the book's target audience. Or, instead of a quote, you notice the wording "with a foreword by" and then the name of a prominent professional.

Next you flip the book over and scan the back-cover copy—the description of the book's features. If you're still interested, you'll thumb through the opening pages. You'll browse a few of the full-length testimonials there, the table of contents with chapter titles that reveal detailed solutions the book will provide, and finally you'll turn to chapter one and read the first paragraphs, maybe a page or two. If all five of those parts of the book excite you, you'll purchase the book.

You'll follow the same basic process if you see stacks of books for sale on tables at a seminar.

Another scenario—you search online for a book that contains the information you want.

No matter how you search for the book you need, you put it through the same basic scrutiny before you buy it.

So, five parts of a book will sell it to a potential reader:
1. The cover—title, book-cover art, subtitle, one-line testimonial or foreword contributor
2. Back-cover copy
3. Testimonials—those that appear on the front and back covers, and those inside the book
4. Table of contents
5. Chapter one's first paragraphs, maybe a page or two—the writing itself

Now your prospect purchases the book, takes it home (or has it shipped, or downloads the e-copy), and begins to read. At this point the second factor, enthusiastic word-of-mouth referrals, will decide the book's subsequent success, and the impact the book will have on your business.

As you can imagine, your book's internal content must be exceptional.

**How you develop, organize, write, and display the internal content determines the results your book will produce** for the reader who purchased it, and whether he recommends it to his friends and colleagues. This also determines whether he will purchase your next book or your other products and advance into your new-business funnel via this juicy bait.

Since both the initial book sales and the book sales that result from those—and the book sales that result from *those*—depend on your published product thrilling its readers in every way, your work on the manuscript must begin with careful planning.

And because your ultimate goal is to draw new customers or clients to your business, each element of your planning needs to target your prospects. So let's begin to plan.

# Thousand-Dollar Tip

Have you ever said this: "You *have* to read this book! The cover isn't all that great, but the information is the best I've ever found on the subject"?

Most of us have. Many books with poor cover designs but exceptional content often sell well. What does this mean for you?

Exceptional content will generate word-of-mouth referrals. A great book cover won't. Make your content the best it can be.

That said, a book cover that captures the eye is an important key to the initial sale.

# Chapter 2

# Develop Your Concept
# to Target Your Prospects

Throughout your years in business, you've accumulated vast knowledge specific to your field. Now your goal is to write a book that will draw droves of fresh prospects to your door.

Perhaps you see your newness to book writing as a disadvantage. After all, you might be familiar with copywriting, but book writing is another animal. Book writing uses different techniques than copywriting because the reason the audience is reading is different, and so the way they read is likewise different. Book writing is not sales writing. Sales writing—style and content—is designed to sell a product or service. Book writing—style and content—is designed to provide solutions the reader can immediately implement.

If you do see your newness to book writing as a disadvantage, I can assure you it isn't. From this point forward, I'll show you how to combine your knowledge with top-selling book-writing strategies, and turn any perceived disadvantage into a highly profitable advantage.

We'll begin by developing the concept you have for your book, the first step of your plan. Think of your plan as your project blueprint.

## Thousand-Dollar Tip

Make the most efficient use of your time. Set aside two months of evenings and Saturdays in which to complete your book. If you allow gaps of time between writing sessions, you'll forget where you were and waste valuable time repeatedly rereading previous material.

# 1. Your Brand

What makes branding so powerful?

"A brand is more than a name. A true brand cannot be copied because a true brand is more than a product. It is a promise, a reflection of the entrepreneur's body, mind, and spirit. . . . If you keep your promise and give people the same things you want, you may be one of the few entrepreneurs who turns their business into a brand." (Source: Robert T. Kiyosaki, *Midas Touch* (coauthor: Donald Trump), (Scottsdale, AZ: Plata Publishing, 2011).)

Your brand is your *promise* to your customers, the promise of what you will deliver—the product as well as its quality. It is also the unique *experience* your customers have with you, the experience you provide. That experience can be professional, personal, funny, extravagant, or anything innate to you that leaves a lingering, positive impression, both in the mind and in the heart of your customer.

In simplest terms, branding is the art of making a distinctive and genuine promise and providing a distinctive experience for those your business serves.

It is also the art of doing so long term.

Each contact your customer has with you builds a perception of your brand, until that brand becomes for them the consistent promise and experience that you always deliver.

So then, what makes branding so powerful? Great brands—product, service, and the experience they give us—earn our loyalty, and inspire us to recommend that business to others.

What does this mean for your book?

Your book must be an extension of your business's singular and genuine promise, as well as the particular experience your business provides, *whether professional, personal, funny, extravagant, or anything unique to you that leaves a lingering, positive impression, both in the mind and in the heart of your customer.*

Incorporate your brand (promise and experience) into your book via the tone and style you write with (the emotional and intellectual level that you communicate on as an entrepreneur), as well as the choice of words you use.

I'll refer to this use of the word *brand* frequently throughout this book. Why? Because your own book is the first experience many prospects will have with you. Your book is the first step toward targeting the prospects you most want to do business with—those who most want to do business with you . . . which means with your distinguishing brand.

## 2. Your Target Readers

Who is your target reader?

Naturally, he is the premium prospect—gender, age, income level, and all related demographics—whom you want to hook and reel into your business.

When you began your business, you researched and pinpointed your target customer's demographics. Use that same information now to fix in your mind precisely who you're writing your book for.

That might sound obvious, but it needs to be underscored. You don't want to bait your hook for salmon, trout, or bass if what you want to catch is swordfish.

The content you put in your book, and the tone, style, and word choice that you write with, will determine the fish you hook for your business.

## 3. Your Book's Content

You might already know what information you will include in your book. If not, consider the size and interests (or needs) of the audience you will be marketing to. Will you be marketing to everyone (general-interest book content such as exercise, nutrition)? To a common-interest group (football fans, antique car collectors, Civil War reenactors, watercolor artists)? Or to an occupational or business niche (homeowners who can't get stains out of their carpets, entrepreneurs who want to write business books)?

Next consider, What is that audience mad or frustrated about? What scares them? What thoughts wake them up at night? (Nothing motivates like fear.) What hobby or interest are they passionate about? What need do they have that no one is providing a solution for?

Or pinpoint the solutions you have in your arsenal that differentiates you—and places you apart from—your competitors.

If you're uncertain which solutions your prospects need, simply ask your customers or clients what information they most come to you for, or would like to see you provide. Or, post a poll at your business Web site and plainly ask visitors what solutions you provide that they use most, and what other solutions they would most like to see you provide. This is also an excellent opportunity to make note of any ideas they supply that you can use to expand your business.

To make sure your book is successful bait, make sure it is bait (content) your prospects want. Need. Are hungry for. What your current customers want most from you will likewise be the bait that will lure your prospects.

Of course, you don't want to put everything you know into your book. The goal is to get the prospect to come to you for further assistance.

Also ask yourself, "What else does my reader want to get out of my book? In addition to solutions, perhaps a chuckle, a dose of inspiration, a weight lifted from their shoulders?" What fits your specific audience?

Once you have an idea of the *basic* content—information, solution(s), experience—your book will provide, then read on.

## 4. Define Your Concept

When you initially planned your business, you wrote down your mission statement, the specific mission you envisioned for your future business coupled with the unique solutions you intended to provide to your customers or clients. Essentially, this mission statement would be the professional promise you would make to your customers and to yourself.

With it, you defined your concept for the business, including your brand.

This is the basic structure of a mission statement:

To use my _____ (knowledge/abilities)
to _____ (what you promise to do/your brand)
for _____ (describe your target customers)
so that _____ (how your target customers will benefit).

Now, using a similar structure, write down your mission statement for your book. In other words, define your concept:

## MISSION STATEMENT FOR MY BOOK

To use my _____
(specific knowledge or abilities)

to produce a book that will _____

_____
(what you promise to do; include wording to reflect your brand)

for _____
(describe your target readers)

so that _____.
(how your target readers will benefit)

Book Mission Statement. Feel free to photocopy and fill out.

Before you picked up a copy of *Business Gold*, you already had an idea that you wanted to write a book about ___ (fill in the blank). You also knew who your target reader would be—your business prospects. Now that you've written out the details for yourself, including how your target readers will benefit from your book, you have provided yourself with an end goal to focus on every moment that you develop your book.

To be sure you achieve that end goal, I recommend keeping your mission statement for your book where you can see it while you write the manuscript.

In order to ensure enthusiastic word-of-mouth referrals and the readers' advancement into your business funnel, how the reader will benefit from your book must remain your primary fixation. That's so important, I'll say it again: With every aspect of developing your book, work to benefit the reader.

If while developing your book you instead fixate on using your book to benefit your business, rather than focus primarily on how to benefit your reader, book sales will not result.

This point cannot be overemphasized.

Your goal is not to promote your business or products or services, at least not overtly. Your goal for the book is to deliver solutions to your reader, just as in business you deliver solutions to your customer.

Eventually you can insert subtle plugs for your business, and I'll show you how. But your book's main focus, especially during the first several chapters, must be solving your readers' problems and fulfilling your readers' needs.

You'll see those two words more often than any other phrase in this book: *the reader*. Always concentrate on how your readers will benefit. The reader is your future customer and also your networking tool. Your book should be an information-rich gift to readers, one they will rave about.

The reader is the star.

## Back-Cover Copy

To help you pinpoint which information to include in your book, write your book's back-cover copy next. When finished, it will sum up your book's content and its benefits to the reader.

It will also inspire your unit, chapter, and section titles as well as the specific information that will appear in each.

The average reader spends less than fifteen seconds scanning a book's back cover. So, include only the most compelling information in order to hook your prospect into looking inside to read more. To do that, the copy must be brief, punchy, and provide only the main benefits or solutions your readers want.

Here's how to structure and write it.

## Headline

Begin with a short, one-sentence **headline** (a question or a statement) that captures your target reader. It should spotlight the potential reader's biggest problem or frustration—the primary solution that your potential reader needs and that your book will provide.

With that first line, you want your potential reader to think, *"This is the book I've been searching for!"*

Your headline should compel them to *need* the book.

If you excite your potential reader with that first question or statement, he will read more, or most, of the back cover. When done well, the headline alone goes a long way toward securing the sale.

Read the back-cover headlines of your favorite business books. Analyze which headlines are the most compelling and why. Use that knowledge to inspire your headline.

Take all the time you need to create a strong, descriptive, compelling question or statement.

Here is more to consider before you begin to write your back-cover copy.

## Summary Paragraph

*"This* is the book I've been searching for!"

Continue to convince your potential reader of that with each subsequent line.

Beneath the headline, in a **summary paragraph** of four concise sentences or fewer (you can add one or two more sentences if writing for discerning entrepreneurs and other business professionals), describe the main benefits or solutions your book will provide.

Provide great information fast. If you *can* summarize the book in one short paragraph, or even one sentence, do it.

Show the potential reader that the book provides valuable information worth far more than the amount they will invest in the book. Pinpoint the advantage of time, money, or other benefits the reader will either save or gain as a result of this purchase.

## Bulleted List

Beneath the summary paragraph, use a **bulleted list** to briefly detail the other top benefits or solutions readers will gain.

## Summary Line

Add a final **summary line** that delivers a compelling burst of excitement for the potential reader.

## To Sum Up

Keep the potential reader engaged by using short paragraphs, short sentences, and bulleted points.

**Try to complete all of the above back-cover copy in 150 words or fewer.**

Since this is one of your primary selling points, invest the time to make it the best you can. Later in *Business Gold*, we'll revise it if needed.

## Write the Back-Cover Copy

Write your back-cover copy now. It'll help you focus your efforts as you develop your book.

# One-Line Book Summary

In the same way you developed a one-line summary for your business and products or services (your elevator pitch), take time now to create an effective one-line summary of your book—its subject matter, audience, and benefits—in any order that best captures attention and compels your listener to *need* your book.

Try to limit the summary to thirty words or fewer. Use the bottom three lines of your book's mission statement, if that would be a powerful elevator pitch.

## ONE-LINE BOOK SUMMARY
### (ELEVATOR PITCH)

One-Line Book Summary. Feel free to photocopy and fill out for your book.

Write your one-line summary now.

Next, read over your book pitch several times and become familiar with it. When someone asks you what your book will be about, you can tell them and begin promoting your book now, even before you publish it.

You should also be able to use this summary in your marketing campaign.

# 5. Develop Your Concept

You might already have a few hundred pages of notes in the form of seminar transcripts, white papers, blog posts, articles that you own the rights to, and the like, ready to be compiled into a book. If so, read through your documents, and while you're reading, on a separate sheet of paper or in a new word-processing document, make a list of all the main topics and subtopics you have. These are the topics you will organize to become the chapters and sections of your book. The solutions that you will provide for your readers.

If you do not yet have written information ready to compile, write or keyboard the main topics and subtopics you want to include in your book, as the topics occur to you, *in no particular order*. This frees the creative mind to rapidly brainstorm ideas without stopping to speculate on organization. We'll organize them later. Again, these are the solutions you'll provide to your readers.

As you list your topics, keep it simple. Permit yourself to note each topic and subtopic using only a few words if you wish, instead of complete sentences.

Plan for approximately ten to twenty main topics, more or fewer if needed. These main topics will become your chapters, one chapter per main topic.

What if you have less than ten topics, you ask? You can write a book that has as little as one main topic, as long as the finished print book is at least forty-nine interior pages in length (fifty-one pages total, including the covers). That's UNESCO's international standard. A non-periodical publication that has fewer than forty-nine interior pages is considered a pamphlet.

That said, if your published book has fewer than one hundred pages and therefore a narrow spine, it could disappear among more commanding books on a shelf.

On the other hand, a book of more than three hundred pages might be costly to produce, and therefore costly for a potential buyer to purchase. If you have enough content to fill significantly more than 350 pages, consider that two books could lead to two times the exposure.

So again, plan for approximately ten to twenty main topics.

Write down your topics and subtopics now—all the ideas that come to you, even if you end up not using them all. (Save those for another book or for magazine articles or blog posts.)

I'll wait here.

## Research Your Competitors

Welcome back. Now that you have your list of topics, it's time to research published books that have content and target readers similar to yours, so that you can further define your particular writing and selling niche.

Research inside your favorite bookstore and/or online; www.BarnesAndNoble.com is an excellent resource for this. At their Web site, simply search books by subject, then sort the results by "Best Selling" (the best-selling books first). You can also research at www.Amazon.com and by keyword searches.

When you locate books with subject matter similar to yours, study each book's title, subtitle or front-cover description, cover testimonials, back-cover copy, table of contents, plus the overview/book description provided online.

As you read, ask yourself: "How does each of these books' textual content and/or target readers differ from mine? What new information can my book deliver that none of these books provides? Or, What distinctive angle can I use that these authors have not used?"

While you research online, be sure to bookmark the Web page of each book you find that is similar to yours. We'll refer back to those Web pages later when we brainstorm ideas for other aspects of your book.

Following is a chart—"Competitor Book Research Sheet"—that you can print out and fill in for each competitor book you research. Research all the books you can find that have content similar to yours.

Be sure to fill in all of the information on the chart. You'll need it all later.

If the chart on the following page is too small, a larger version is available in the Bonus! section near the end of the book.

Do your competitor research now. When you are finished, use the research sheets' combined information to plan your book's niche.

*How?* you ask. On the bottom of each **Competitor Book Research Sheet**, you filled in the space "How my book's audience and/or content will be unique." On a fresh piece of paper or new word-processing document, compile those notes to answer the questions:

- "How does each of these books' textual content and/or target readers differ from mine?"
- "What new information can my book deliver that none of these books provides?"
- Or, "What unique angle can I use that these authors have not used?"

Do this once you have completed your competitor research, and you'll have a clear blueprint for how your book will stand out from your competitors'.

# Competitor Book Research Sheet

## Front Cover

| | |
|---|---|
| Book title: | |
| Subtitle (if any): | |
| Edition: | |
| Author(s): | |
| Endorser/Foreword contributor: | |
| Soft or hard cover: | |
| Book cover color/ design/illustrations: | |

## Back Cover

| | |
|---|---|
| Main topics (content) according to the back-cover copy: | |
| Target audience: | |
| Retail price: | |

## Inside

| | |
|---|---|
| Publisher: | |
| Copyright year: | |
| Number of pages: | |
| Attention-grabbing chapter titles: | |
| How my book's audience and/or content will be unique: | |

## Revise Your Topics

So, you've defined your book's concept with a mission statement, back-cover copy, and a one-line book summary (elevator pitch). You've also researched published books that have content and target readers similar to yours and determined your book's unique niche.

Now, revise the list of your book's topics to reflect the new information your book will deliver that none of those books has provided, and/or the distinctive angle you will use that those authors have not used. Remove unnecessary topics from your list and add any new topics to your list.

As you revise your topics, be sure to keep uppermost in your mind the needs of your target audience, the prospects for your business funnel. Make certain the topics will give your readers the solutions they need.

See you when you come back.

## Organize Your Topics

"So, how do I organize my topics?"

Great question, and here's the answer. As I mentioned a few pages ago, each chapter should contain one main point and its related subpoints. You might find a simple outline useful as you plot the order in which you will present your topics and subtopics.

On a new word-processor page, write your simple outline of topics and subtopics in a logical progression. The following may seem obvious, but many authors find the reminder helpful: Be sure to explain how to hold the proverbial golf club before you teach them how to swing it. In other words, develop each point in a way that is easy for the reader to understand. Simple concepts first, then more complex concepts after.

Is topic organization difficult to do in your word-processing document? Then simply write each topic and subtopic on its own index card. Index cards are easy to reorder, and they are an effective way to envision your book's layout.

If you plan to write a biographical business book, you may opt for a chronological ordering of your topics. (We'll talk about writing a business biography in more detail in Chapter 7.)

If you brainstormed topics that won't fit well in your book, just save them for your next book, or use them as topics of magazine articles or blog posts.

When you are finished with your outline, you will have an organized, working copy of your table of contents, the blueprint for your manuscript.

Here's an example of part of a fictitious book outline:

---

### Defeat Your Dragon ~ How to Conquer FEAR
(^working title or main concept^)

I.  Chapter One: Two Kinds of Fear
    A.  Helpful ~ Suit-of-Armor Fear
        1)  Safety—Move! You're about to get hit by a car!
        2)  Choices—Consider carefully before you say "I do" personally or professionally
    B.  Hindering ~ Fire-Breathing-Dragon Fear
        1)  The voice that whispers "can't" and self-doubt in your ear
        2)  FEAR—Fake Evidence that Appears Real
II.  Chapter Two: Two Kinds of Swords to Slay Your FEAR Dragon
    A.  The Dream Is Mightier than the Dragon
    B.  The Secret Sword Everyone Possesses

---

Sample topic organization.

As you can see, this organization of topics begins by teaching the basics of the subject matter, then advances toward detailed solutions.

Teach them to hold the club before you teach them to swing it. Help them to walk, then to run.

Good news—I've run out of clichés. I'll see you after you organize your topics.

## 6. Create Your Book Title

This is where manuscript development gets ultra exciting. Maybe you've already started brewing ideas for your book title. Since you have a book mission statement and table of contents in hand, you can now affix a title to the manuscript. Add a subtitle if needed.

Considerations? Foremost: The main title should describe your book's content as clearly as possible.

If I'd titled this book simply *Gold*, potential readers would've had no idea if the book was about gold stock investments, designing gold jewelry, or a novel about the 1849 California Gold Rush. Few people would have bothered to pick it up off the store shelf. Online, potential readers search "how to write a business book." Therefore, the title *Business Gold: How to Write a Book to Spotlight Your Expertise, Attract a Ton of New Customers, and Explode Your Profits!* tells a potential reader that this book will show them how to write a book to add serious profits to their businesses.

Also, your main title should:
- be memorable
- be easy to say (so that readers can easily refer the book to friends and associates)
- impact and excite the reader
- target your readers/prospects (the main title of this book is **Business** *Gold*—clearly it is written for business professionals)
- reflect your brand

With all those considerations, your muse might not kick out a title immediately. Perhaps not even until you're about to publish the book. No worries. Having the title nailed down enables a writer to brainstorm chapter and section titles and ideas for graphics, but oftentimes chapter and section titles and ideas for graphics will inspire the book title.

Remember the competitor research you did? Let those book titles inspire ideas for yours. Of course, be sure your book title is distinctly unique.

Write down all of your ideas, even if they're just single words or concepts. Feel free to ask your colleagues and trusted customers for their opinions.

Creating the title is one of the hardest parts of producing a book, and one of the most important—remember, it's the means you'll use to first hook potential readers—but gradually the right title will come to you.

Now, pour yourself a caffeinated cup of instant energy, and brainstorm your book title.

## 7. Create Chapter and Section Titles

Now that you have an idea what your book title might be, go over your topic outline once more. For each topic and subtopic, create a chapter or section title. Much like the book title, each title should:

- succinctly and accurately convey the topic
- impact and excite the reader
- target your readers/prospects
- reflect your brand

Yes, unless you're gifted with titles, this too will likely take a little time. If so, no worries. Sleep on it, more than once, if needed. In addition to engaging your reader, each title should also inspire you to write gripping, valuable content. Adjust each title until it wows you.

Feel free to revisit the competitor research you did, the Web pages you bookmarked. Let those chapter and section titles (found in each book's table of contents) inspire ideas for yours. Again, be sure your titles are distinctly unique.

If one or more titles do not come to you within a few days, move forward to the next step and simply use the topic description from your outline. When the chapter or section title finally comes to you, insert it then.

See you when you're done.

# 8. Choose Your Book Style

Welcome back.

So, what do I mean by "book style"? I mean, How do you want to deliver your concepts? In what format will you write the content?

Now you might be thinking, "Which book styles can I choose from?" Anticipating that question, I've listed the top three book styles most business-book authors use, beginning with the most common, and key information about each of the three.

### 1. Informational/How To

- This is the most commonly used format for business books. *Business Gold* is the informational/how-to style of book.
- This structure works well for both B2B and B2C content.
- Information is clearly presented, in straightforward terms, enabling the reader to immediately apply the solutions.
- In addition to presenting information gleaned from personal experience and/or in-depth research, the author may use brief stories/parables (true or fictional), anecdotes, charts, graphs, illustrations, photographs, one-page cartoons, callout (text) boxes, and/or other graphics to convey data and its relevance, in any way the author chooses in order to achieve his goals for the book and reader.
- Informational/how-to books can be any length, but word count typically falls between 15K and 70K.

## 2. Business Biography

- This is less commonly used than the informational/how-to format. *Rich Dad, Poor Dad* and *Midas Touch* are business biographies.
- This structure can work for both B2B and B2C content.
- Information is clearly presented, in straightforward terms, based on and described via the author's personal experiences and that of his associates and mentors, enabling the reader to immediately apply the solutions.
- In addition to presenting information gleaned from personal experience, that of his associates and mentors, and/or in-depth research, the author may use brief stories/parables (true or fictional), anecdotes, charts, graphs, illustrations, photographs, one-page cartoons, callout (text) boxes, and/or other graphics to convey data and its relevance, in any way the author chooses in order to achieve his goals for the book and reader. Authors of biographies tend to make lesser use of these tools than do authors of informational/how-to books. Instead, the primary focus of a biography is on the story itself and the solutions it provides.
- Biographies can be any length, but word count typically falls between 30K and 70K.
- A business biography is recommended if you are a celebrity or have an established audience of thousands and have highly in-demand information to convey.
- Because of the biography's unique characteristics and the level of expertise required to write it successfully, I encourage all who wish to choose business biography as their book style to gain editorial assistance from a manuscript editor/ghostwriter who possesses proven know-how with writing business biographies. I'll discuss working with a manuscript editor later in the book.

## 3. Allegory

- This is a less common, but often popular, format used to deliver individual or a few select business concepts. Thus, allegories are typically much shorter than other business-book styles. *Who Moved My Cheese?* and *The One Minute Manager* are allegories. An allegory is a fictional story that uses symbolic fictional characters (often not human) and objects to convey truths in order to benefit the reader.

- This structure works well for both B2B and B2C content.

- Information is creatively presented, in pictorial terms, to lead readers to useful conclusions.

- In addition to presenting information within a creative, fictional story, authors of allegories often make use of one-page cartoons and similar illustrations in order to achieve their goals for the book and reader.

- Allegories are commonly less than 20K words in length.

- Because of the allegory's unique characteristics and the high level of expertise required to write it successfully, I strongly encourage all who wish to choose allegory as their book style to gain editorial assistance from a manuscript editor/ghostwriter who possesses proven fictional and allegorical know-how. I'll discuss working with a manuscript editor later in the book.

Those are the top three book styles nonfiction authors use to achieve the highest sales numbers and the best results for their readers. However, you are not limited to those options. When choosing your book style, consider your brand and goals, as well as the best way to target your reader, the prospect you wish to draw into your business. Your book style may be one of the above, or a format that is original, though I recommend that authors adhere to the same book style for any subsequent books they write.

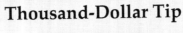

## Thousand-Dollar Tip

Need help deciding the best book style for your needs and goals? See the Bonus! section at the end of the book for a special coaching offer, then visit www.BusinessBookProductions.com/Coach.

In Chapters 6, 7, and 8, I'll teach you how to construct and write your manuscript using each one of the three book styles.

Take time now to decide which book style will work best for your goals. Keep that style in mind as you continue to read.

# Part 2

# Write the Manuscript

# Chapter 3

# 6 Secret Strategies to Jumpstart Your Muse

If you're a church-goer, you might have heard the Bible verse Romans 12:6—"We have different gifts, according to the grace given to each of us" (*NIV*). When we're born, God gives each person a distinctive gift, an ability (or two) that we do especially well and find satisfaction in. I love to sing and dance, but do both with the savvy of a yowling three-legged frog on an oil slick. Since God pointedly deprived me of those talents, at least in any marketable way, you are enjoying the magnificent publication now before you.

I'm a writer and editor by nature. That's my gift. Sitting down to write a book doesn't intimidate me like it can non-writers. I can't shut my muse off. It bombards me with ideas 24/7. My mind writes while I'm driving. It writes while I'm walking the dog. It writes while I'm trying to sleep.

You've spent your career becoming an expert at what you do. I fully understand that that doesn't mean you consider yourself ready to crack your knuckles and type out a manuscript.

If you have trouble jumpstarting your muse, here are six secret strategies many of my clients find advantageous. As a novelist, I used these techniques to write 75,000- to 100,000-word novels, from first page to last, in less than six weeks each.

## Jumpstart Your Muse Secret Strategy #1: Time, Place, and Freedom

When you sit down to work on your manuscript, allocate two to three hours (more, if you write on weekends) in which you will not be interrupted. Zero distractions. No family, no Internet, no phones, no dog. Free yourself (your muse) from all other responsibilities. Before you begin, plan the writing schedule you will follow, and let your family know what to expect in the coming weeks, or they'll be plotting your computer's demise before you're done.

Be sure to schedule your most alert time for writing, the time of day when you feel the most motivated. Also, write *where* you feel most motivated to write.

Larger blocks of dedicated time means your muse will be freed, and inspired, to do its thing. Too, your book will be completed sooner and sending new clients to your business.

## Jumpstart Your Muse Secret Strategy #2: Write the Topic That Excites You

From your list of chapter titles, choose the topic you feel most excited to write about, and begin there. Don't feel that you have to write linearly, meaning in the order the topics will appear in your book. That can put a damper on your inspiration to write. It'll bore you.

And if it bores you to write it, it'll bore the reader to read it.

Instead, each time you sit down to create content, free yourself to write whichever topic appeals to you to write. Or work on the topic for which you have the most notes completed. That will inspire your muse and make the writing go fast.

## Jumpstart Your Muse Secret Strategy #3:
## MP3 Recorder

A quality MP3 recorder is one of the few tools a writer cannot do without. If you have a recorder that you use for business, invest in another one to use exclusively for writing. It will be the most valuable item you purchase other than this book.

Keep your recorder with you at all times. And I do mean *all* times. When an author is in writing mode, book ideas can strike anytime, anywhere. Keep the recorder with you so you can easily note your ideas.

If you don't, you'll kick yourself for it later when you can't remember what you'd wanted to say.

When you sit down to write, start your session by playing back the recorded notes. If possible, do not outsource the note-typing to a transcriptionist. Type the recorded notes into your word processor personally. This further helps to accelerate the creative flow, since typing recorded ideas generates even more ideas. A couple of brief, recorded notes can easily inspire several paragraphs of great content.

## Jumpstart Your Muse Secret Strategy #4:
## Transform Writer's Block into a Writing Boom

How can a writer avoid the infamous "block"? Simple. At the end of each writing day, decide what you're going to write about the next day. This enables your mind to stockpile ideas for when you sit down to write.

Record every idea in your MP3 recorder.

When you do sit down, you know what you're going to write about, and, as noted in Strategy #3, typing the playback will inspire more ideas still. A boom!

## Jumpstart Your Muse Secret Strategy #5:
## Switch Off the Editor

Some people new to writing books think that editing while you write is an efficient use of time. In fact, the opposite is true.

Writing is a creative process. Right brain. Editing is logical. Left brain. Like an electrical switch, only one can receive current at a time.

If you try to throw the switch to editor mode at the same the writer is switched on, that causes writer's block. It stops the creative flow.

Constantly trying to flip the switch back and forth from writer to editor to writer again slows the creative flow to a trickle. In the end, writing takes far longer.

It's faster and you get better results by writing a rough first draft, then *re*writing to make the content shine like gold.

## Jumpstart Your Muse Secret Strategy #6:
## Seventh-Inning Stretch

When writing for long periods—several hours or all day—take breaks when you need them. There's no sense ending each day feeling like you've been dragged by a horse, especially if you're the one whipping its backside. Take a short walk. Get some coffee and chat with your spouse or a friend. Creativity needs breathing space, or you'll choke your muse.

# Chapter 4

## More Ideas to Jumpstart Your Muse: Interview with Author's Coach Ann McIndoo

If you *still* have trouble getting words onto the page, then you might choose to connect with an author's coach. Also known as a writing coach, this professional can help you to jumpstart your muse and get your words onto the page.

Meet Ann McIndoo. She is Your Author's Coach who, through her successful books and coaching programs, assists stumped non-writers to further develop their book concepts, get their words onto the page, and quickly produce the first draft of their manuscripts.

As CEO and founder of So, You Want to Write!, Ann helps writers to get their books out of their heads. Designed for professionals, entrepreneurs, business owners, coaches, and CEOs, Ann's coaching takes writers through a proven process and helps them to achieve their book-writing goals.

Her own books include *7 Easy Steps to Write Your Book: How to Get Your Book Out of Your Head and a Manuscript In Your Hands!*, *7*

*Easy Steps to Write Your Book: Author's Journal*, and *So, You Want to Write!*

Since 2005, Ann has helped produce more than four hundred books for professionals and entrepreneurs. Some of her clients include Tony Robbins, Bob Proctor, Mark Victor Hansen, and Dan Poynter. She teaches the following:

- How to Prepare yourself to write—what to do *before* you pick up your pen!
- How to Organize your material—turn that pile of notes into a real book!
- How to Produce content for your book—start writing!
- How to Stay Motivated and deal with procrastination and writer's block!
- Amazing Writing technologies—simple, effective ways to produce content quickly!

and more.

The following is transcribed from a live interview and lightly edited for easy reading. Ann's organizational techniques work best for the informational/how-to book style, but many of her additional strategies work well for all authors.

**Tammy Barley:** Ann, welcome! We're excited to have you with us!

**Ann McIndoo:** It's my pleasure!

**Tammy Barley:** Can you tell us a little bit more about what you do?

**Ann McIndoo:** Sure. Well, in addition to helping an entrepreneur or business professional get their book out of their head, I help them create their ancillary products—their workbook, journals, audio program—ancillary products to help them generate additional revenue.

As you know, when you have a book, you can sell it for fifteen dollars; however, if you have a book and a workbook—or a book, a workbook, and an audio program—now you can sell your product for a lot more, because you have added so much value to the package.

**Tammy Barley:** In your book *7 Easy Steps to Write Your Book: How to Get Your Book Out of Your Head and a Manuscript In Your Hands!*, you note that during your years as Your Author's Coach, you have found three ingredients to be essential to developing a successful book. I'll paraphrase:

1. The book's content must be unique, different from what has already been published.
2. The book must deliver value to the reader far beyond the purchase price.
3. The book must provide solutions to the reader and help him to achieve measurable results.

How should writers accomplish these?

**Ann McIndoo:** Yes, these are the three ingredients for developing a successful book—your content must be different from what has already been published, the book must deliver value, and you must provide some solutions in your book. Now, you don't have to give all the solutions in your book, but enough to get them engaged and wanting more.

I typically like to recommend, if you have The Five Secrets to ___ (fill in the blank), to put at least two of them in your book, and put the other three in your workbook. Writers can accomplish this by spreading out their material. Here's how I like to say it. Put your general content in your book, your details in your workbook, and your nitty-gritty in your audio program.

So, in the book, you give them a little bit. You give them the *what* and a little bit of the *how*. But in the workbook and the audio program, then you give them the rest of the *how*, how to get everything done.

Not putting it all in your book is one way you can accomplish getting people into your funnel, keeping them in your funnel, and taking them through the whole journey.

**Tammy Barley:** In *7 Easy Steps to Write Your Book*, the first six chapters—half the book—guides the reader through **Step 1: Prepare to Write Your Book**. Many writers already have concepts for their books, and dozens of content ideas as well. Why is preparation so important?

**Ann McIndoo:** That's a great question. Preparation is the foundation. Preparation is the most important thing you can do with anything. Whether you're writing a book, or playing golf, or baking brownies, preparation is everything.

When you bake a cake, what do you do? You get out your mix, get out your ingredients, preheat the oven, and you get ready to put everything in that bowl, mix it up, pour it in a pan, and throw it into the oven. You prepare.

Think of anything. Whether you're painting your house, or you're playing golf this Saturday, you do things to prepare so that you can make it the best event ever, so that you can achieve success in whatever you're doing.

It's the same thing with a book. And that's why step one of my book is to create your resource pile—to gather everything that inspires you or reminds you about what you're going to write about in your book. It doesn't have to be in any order. Preparation is about creating that resource pile, and it's just gathering, gathering, gathering. It doesn't matter what that pile looks like. And that's why preparation is so important, so that you know exactly what you have, and you also know what you don't have, before you start writing your book.

**Tammy Barley:** What do you consider to be important to add to the resource pile?

**Ann McIndoo:** The resource pile can be anything—journals, books, memorabilia, a postcard, a gift you've received as a thank you—anything. The resource pile can be made up of anything tangible, you know, paper, books, magazines, anything.

It can also be made of intangible things, a memory, an experience, a thought in your head, an idea in your heart, anything you have that you want to talk about. All of those are items that will be put in your resource pile.

Preparation includes creating your resource pile.

Chapter two of my book, creating your *chapter* piles. And then creating your Manuscript Grid™. And taking all the steps that I talk about throughout the book—that is preparation. All the way through chapter eight or nine when you actually talk, or write, your book. You are preparing to write your book.

**Tammy Barley:** The Manuscript Grid is the tool you've developed which writers can use to detail and structure their books' content, essentially the blueprint they will use to write their books, and it's more than a simple outline. Could you explain how the Manuscript Grid can speed up and simplify the actual writing?

**Ann McIndoo:** Absolutely. Lots of people just sit down, and they say, okay I want to write my book, and they sit down at their computer, and they have a white screen, a brand-new document in front of them. And then they're like, "Hmm, what did I want to talk about? What should I say first? How do I lead into that?" And they sit there for an hour trying to figure out what they're going to say.

And so the Manuscript Grid, which is something I created based on creating the resource pile and the chapter piles, is the structure to your book. Just like building a house. If you have a floor plan, you know exactly where the foundation lays down, where the walls go, where the plumbing is, where your bathroom and your kitchen are going to be, because you have the floor plan. You have a blueprint. The Manuscript

Grid is the blueprint for your book. It speeds up and simplifies the actual talking or writing of your book because it gives you the subjects, it gives you the topics, and it gives you the order you're going to speak or write about them in. That's how it speeds it up and makes it easy.

**Tammy Barley:** (As a side note to readers, The Manuscript Grid does this both vertically and horizontally, often on a single page, so you can actually see the concise layout of your book. It's a nifty tool.) Ann, you also developed three Writer's Power Tools™ which inspire stumped writers (my expression) to begin putting words on the page. How did you develop these tools?

**Ann McIndoo:** (Laughs.) That's a great question. First let me give you a quick, simple definition of what I consider the difference between a writer and an author. In my authors coaching program, I've encountered many people who say, "I'm not a writer. How am I ever going to get this book done?" That led me to figure out that there's a difference between a writer and an author. A writer is someone who writes on a consistent basis and makes money from the writing, whether it's an article, or a blog, or social media, but they write. They write every day and they get paid for their writing.

An author is someone who's taken their material, organized it, and put it in a book. And I have found that when I explain this to my clients, I hear a big sigh of relief. "Oh, okay."

Now there are some people who love to write, but for the most part the professionals, the entrepreneurs I work with, are not writers. They're businesspeople. And there's a significant difference there.

So now, how did I develop these tools? Well, as you may know, I worked with Tony Robbins for more than ten years. I worked very closely with him, and I saw that he did certain things to get ready to work. He has what he calls a power move—he gets his body ready—and I took it a couple of steps further.

First, I made the Power Script, which is what's in your head, what you say to yourself before you write, or before you have your writing appointment. If you're saying something like, "Oh I love to write, I can't wait to write, to work on my project, I'm so excited about working on my book," well then of course you're going to have a great session, and your head is ready.

But if you keep telling yourself things like, "Oh, boy, here I am. I'm going to write; I hope it comes out right," or "I don't think I can write this," well then of course you're not going to have a good session.

So I created the Power Script to get your head into the game.

The Power Move I modeled after Tony Robbins, to get your body in that place. You can jump up and down, and clap, and rub your hands together, or you can be really quiet and you can become centered with candles and music, whatever gets your body in the right place.

And then your environment. I call it your Power Anchors, whether it's your desk, or a patio chair next to the pool, or a bench at the park. It's about having that right environment where you can feel inspired to create your book.

And that's how I created the Writer's Power Tools, and I encourage people to use the power tools, because when you start using them, after a while they become a part of you, and you can snap through them in a heartbeat, and you get ready to write instantly.

**Tammy Barley:** It's a kind of conditioning.

**Ann McIndoo:** Yes, absolutely.

You know, about the environment, it's one of the most important things. In fact, it's everything. Here's one of the stories that I like to share. I have all kinds of things on my desk that remind me of different places I've been and writing sessions I've had. One of the most powerful ones that I have is, on one of my trips to Fiji with Tony

Robbins, we were working on his book. We had a great session. It was an amazing session. After we finished, I looked at him and I said, "Wow, that was powerful," and he just smiled and he said, "Well, thank you." And I said, "You know what? I'm going to go for a walk on the beach. Here I am in Fiji, I'm going to go for a walk on the beach." And he said, "You know what? I want to go too."

So here I am, with Tony Robbins, on the beach, walking along the shore in Fiji—it's absolutely spectacular. We stopped and talked, and I was kind of digging my toes in the sand, and I felt a little something pick at my foot. So I bent down and lifted it up, and it was one of the most beautiful seashells. . . . It was beautiful, beautiful, like a mini conch shell. And so I picked it up, rinsed it in the water, and decided right then and there that I was going to bring it home. And I did.

It sits on my desk, and every time I look at it, two things happen. First, I look at it, and I pick it up, and I remember exactly where I was. I remember myself on that beach with Tony Robbins in Fiji. And then the second thing that happens to me when I hold the shell and I touch it, I get that same excited feeling that I had during that writing session. And so that is a very powerful anchor for me.

So that's why I encourage everyone, whether they're writing a book or not, to have a couple of those Power Anchors on their desk, things that remind them of places they've been or things that they've done. It could be a trophy, it could be a certificate, a thank-you note, a button or badge you received at an event. You know, I always buy little doodahs wherever I go because they remind me of things I've done and places I've been, and they bring me into a really great state of happiness and excitement and pleasure, and that helps me to be in that same state for writing.

And so that's why I talk about the Power Anchors and having environment.

**Tammy Barley:** I love that, and I look forward to collecting more of them myself.

44

You know, you mention in your book that once book writing begins, challenges can arise if writers experience long lapses of time between writing sessions (you call sessions Writing Appointments). What challenges come up if they're not able to keep their writing appointments?

**Ann McIndoo:** If you don't keep your writing appointments, what happens is, two things. One, you forget what you're writing about, and two, you lose interest. I think the reason for that is because you don't have a compelling enough future with that book. You have not totally committed.

You must decide, commit, and resolve to get that book done. And you must have a compelling reason why you want that book done. If you're writing it just because you want to write it, you know what? It's going to take you a long time. If you're writing your book because you're going to help people, because it's going to generate revenue— which I highly recommend creating your ancillary products based on your book; now you can create a lot of revenue—then you need to keep that compelling future.

**Tammy Barley:** What is the best way business professionals with demanding schedules can avoid those writing lapses?

**Ann McIndoo:** Oh, that's a wonderful question. You know, one of the things that keeps you moving is taking massive action and having a compelling future. And so one of the things that I do with my authors when we first start, one of the first things that I have them do, is fill out an author's questionnaire—I have them fill out an exercise called a *vision for best outcome*—What is the vision of your book? What is the outcome of your book? What is the purpose of your book? And the reason I have them do that is so that they can write down that compelling reason. Why are you writing this book? To help people?

45

To make a difference? To make money? To find a cure? Whatever it may be.

And so that's the first thing I recommend, so that you have it at your side, you have that right with you. Then if you encounter one of these little bumps, one of these little lapses, or you think, oh I'm not really in the mood—as long as you tell yourself you're not in the mood, then you're not going to be in the mood.

The next thing I do is I have authors make writing appointments. No appointments equals no book. So if you make an appointment once a week, every Wednesday from six to eight, or on Mondays, Tuesdays, and Wednesdays from three to five, I'm going to work on my book. If you have an appointment and you honor it, then the challenges won't even come up, because you are on a schedule.

Success is based on taking action. Success is based on being accountable. Sometimes you have a coach, and that's why lots of people hire me, because I hold them accountable, I'm their coach, I take them through step by step.

And I like to say that you must have the three D's: determination, discipline, and dedication. Those are the three ingredients to have in this project. In any project. So you can put them down on a sticky note, type them up in big letters, and you can put them on your wall to remind you.

And I always like to have authors, in their calendar, pick a color, whether it's blue or green or purple, whatever color they want, and highlight the writing appointments in their calendar, so they can see, that's when I'm working on my book. Writing appointment: chapter one. Writing appointment: Manuscript Grid. Writing appointment: storyboard. Whatever they're working on in their book.

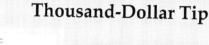

**Thousand-Dollar Tip**

"No writing appointments equals no book. . . .
Success is based on taking action."

—Ann McIndoo

**Tammy Barley:** What techniques can business professionals use to maintain a writing mind-set throughout the hours at work each day?

**Ann McIndoo:** To keep your writing mind-set, use your Writer's Power Tools, your writer's appointments, and those three ingredients: your determination, discipline, and dedication.

**Tammy Barley:** In your book, you talk about Trigger Sentences™. What are those?

**Ann McIndoo:** When you follow my process, you're going to create your resource pile, you're going to create your chapter piles, and you'll do your Manuscript Grid, which is the structure of your book.

Then you're going to create your Trigger Sentences. Each sentence is based on a topic in your book.

First you have your keyword and phrase that you're going to talk about. For instance, let's say chapter one, topic number one is self-esteem. And so the first trigger sentence would be, What are the most important things I want to say about self-esteem? Then perhaps the second topic is, How do I create self-esteem? Then you write a trigger sentence on the most important thing you're going to say about how to create self-esteem.

What you're doing is you're creating sentences based on each topic, sentences that act as springboards to remind you what you're going to write about or talk about when you do your book.

Sometimes people who are not really writers but have content, they write key words and phrases, or they write bullet points. People who *are* writers write a sentence, two sentences; I've gotten Trigger Sentences that are as long as sixty-five pages. So it's up to the individual. I ask for one sentence. People typically do a little bit more than that.

But that trigger sentence is a springboard for creating content.

**Tammy Barley:** In your book, you tell readers they can "talk [their] book in a week." Does this mean they can dictate their book in just seven days? If so, how can they make this happen?

**Ann McIndoo:** Actually, you can talk your book in a day, and I have done it literally hundreds of times with other authors. Talking your book is very easy, especially if you are prepared. If you have your Manuscript Grid, you have the structure. If you have your Trigger Sentences, you have the beginning of your content. If you have your storyboard, you have the layout. You have everything that's going to be in your book.

In my Author's Boot Camp™—I have anywhere between ten and thirty people in each Author's Boot Camp—everybody talks their book in one day. We start talking at about ten in the morning, and typically everybody's done by five or six in the afternoon.

So, how does this happen? (Laughs.) Well, it's because you're prepared. And when you talk your book, it's a lot faster than typing your book. And so when I say you can do it in just seven days, what I'm talking about is, if your book has ten chapters, you can talk a chapter or two once a day. You can set up a writing appointment from, say, eight till ten in the morning, and you talk one or two chapters, maybe three chapters. And every day you have an appointment for a

48

couple of hours, and you talk a couple of chapters. Within a week you have your book.

Obviously, if you talk one chapter a day, then in two weeks you can have your book. But it's very, very simple with a small digital recorder. You can talk your book very quickly. Typically, a 150- to 180-page book takes about four to six hours to talk your book, depending on how fast you speak. Some people speak very slowly, some people speak very quickly, but typically four to six hours.

**Tammy Barley:** I think I already know how you're going to answer my next question, but here goes: In your experience, what are the best ways to overcome writer's block? I'm certain you're going to say *preparation.*

**Ann McIndoo:** (Laughs.) Absolutely! You know, writer's block is fear. In one of the chapters of my book, I list the strategies for busting through writer's block. My favorite strategy—I don't get writers block—but my favorite strategy is when I'm stuck, or I'm not quite sure what to talk about, is to simply start talking about it. Have your digital recorder ready. So if you have a topic, and you don't know what to say about it, just start talking about it. It doesn't matter what you say. So if you want to start talking about fear, What is fear? How come I have fear? How can I get over fear? What really is fear? Just start asking questions. I call other people up and ask them about it. Just start talking about it, and that immediately wipes out any writer's block.

As I say in my book, there is no such thing as writer's block. You know, a lot of people reading this think, "Ah, she doesn't know what she's talking about. She doesn't know *me.*" If you have writer's block, or if you think you have writer's block, it's because there's fear—you don't know what to say about something. So start talking about it, and something will come up, and your writer's block will disappear.

**Tammy Barley:** Fantastic ideas, Ann. Excellent strategies. In *7 Easy Steps to Write Your Book*, you deliver valuable strategies for both first-time and published authors. As Your Author's Coach, you also provide direct assistance to clients through coaching sessions. Of business book writers, who will benefit most from your books, and who will benefit most from working with you personally?

**Ann McIndoo:** My *strategy* works for anyone who wants to write a book, whether they're a professional, a speaker, a consultant, trainers, sales representatives, realtors, leadership, and even students. My process works for anybody who wants to write a book, write a memo, a letter, a book report, create a thesis. . . . I have young authors from nine years old, eleven, fourteen, seventeen-year-old authors. I have business professionals in their forties, fifties, and sixties, and my most experienced author is eighty-nine years old. The process works for anyone.

When you work with me personally, you have your coach—I take you through the steps one by one—and it's a great experience. I love what I do, and I get wonderful letters and testimonials about people's experiences, and whether it's a book for career, for business as a business tool, as an introduction—I like to recommend speakers have books to use as introductions so they can build rapport with their clients. A book can be a business card. A book can be used as a promotional marketing tool. Books are very valuable.

Unfortunately the book itself does not make you very much money, and so my goal is to figure out how *can* a book make you money. And the book can make you money by creating ancillary products and generating revenue based on your book.

A book is always a great thing to do.

**Tammy Barley:** What takes place during the first coaching session?

**Ann McIndoo:** During the first coaching session—I like to call it *Authors, Start Your Engines*. Basically what we do in the first coaching session, I talk about creating your resource pile, I talk about taking on the author's identity, because if you don't have your author's identity, then writing is going to be hard to do. If you keep saying, "I'm not an author. I don't know how to write. I don't know how to do this," you know, it's not going to happen. You take on that author's identity, just like you've taken on the identity of your career, or being a mother, or being a real estate professional. Whatever identity you do have about yourself, when you take that on wholeheartedly, then it serves you. And it's the same thing with an author's identity.

I talk about the author's identity in the first session. I talk about preparing, how to get ready, what to do to get started, to start beginning to work on your book.

**Tammy Barley:** What is the second session like?

**Ann McIndoo:** In the second session we talk about the Manuscript Grid. Now we start getting down to the nitty-gritty.

Actually, the first session and the second session are the hardest and the meatiest. After that, the third through the sixth sessions are very fast.

In the second session, I have you talk about your author's book tour. Everybody needs to go on a personal author's book tour. I encourage the author to go to the bookstore, go to the helper at the bookstore, don't tell them you're writing a book, just ask, "Can you show me where I can find a book on ___," and then describe your topic. And see where the person takes them. Pull out the competition, pull out the books that are the competitors'. Look at them. See what the covers look like. See what the fonts and the pages look like. Look at everything. And they can get ideas about what they want their book to look like, and what they don't want their book to have.

51

And then I encourage people to go to the best-seller rack and look at all the best-sellers. What are the titles? What are the colors? What are the fonts? What do the best-sellers look like? So that can start getting ideas about what your book will look like.

So in session two, we get into the Manuscript Grid, we talk about the subjects, getting the chapters in order, getting the subjects, the topics, and creating the structure for the book. And creating your Manuscript Grid—depending on how you've prepared and how good your resource and chapter piles are, it can take a couple of hours, it usually doesn't take more than four or five hours do the Manuscript Grid. But then now you have the whole structure for your book.

**Tammy Barley:** At your Web site, you tell visitors, "You can go from having a book idea in your head to holding your published book in your hands, in just 10-12 weeks using my unique book-writing process. It's easy, fun, and most importantly, it works!" Ten to twelve weeks. Is this the length of time personal coaching lasts, how long writing lasts by following the 7 Easy Steps in your book, or both? If a writer needs a book faster, do you have a recommendation to help him accomplish that?

**Ann McIndoo:** I have a six-week coaching program. Typically, in six weeks, by the end of week number five, you are ready to talk your book. And so here's how I lay out the twelve weeks.

For the first five weeks, you prepare to talk your book.

The sixth week, you talk your book.

The seventh week, you have it transcribed.

The eighth and ninth week, you do the editing.

The tenth week you get your testimonials, you get your book cover done, you get ready to publish.

Eleventh and twelfth weeks are publishing.

So depending on how long you spend editing, how long it takes to have it transcribed, that could make it take longer, but you could get it done in ten to twelve weeks.

**Tammy Barley:** Do you schedule one coaching session per week?

**Ann McIndoo:** Yes, I usually do one coaching session per week for the first five or six weeks. Then during the transcribing, editing, and publishing, we still talk, but it's like a status call: "How are you doing on this?" or "Show me that." We catch up on the progress of their work. I do guide them and help them, but it's not like the first five weeks where they're actually creating and preparing. In the second six weeks, they're mostly waiting, for the editing, transcribing, and publishing. But it's a really important part of the process.

I like to do once a week with an author, because then we can get done pretty quickly. Because not everybody has a lot of spare time, I usually recommend two to three hours a week that you dedicate to your project: listening to the call, talking with me, doing your homework, usually about three hours a week. Now, not everybody may have three hours a week. They have jobs, they have their families. Then we can do the call every two weeks. I like to do every ten days to two weeks so that we finish in a few months.

**Tammy Barley:** How long does a telephone call generally last?

**Ann McIndoo:** Anywhere from thirty to forty-five minutes. It's short and sweet. It's not long.

**Tammy Barley:** These are individual, one-on-one telephone calls rather than group coaching?

**Ann McIndoo:** Well, here's what I have them do. When you sign up for my office-coaching program, you have access to my authors membership site. You go to the site, and you listen to call number one on your own. Then you do the homework, you send me the homework, and then you talk to me privately. We talk for thirty to forty-five minutes about your homework, about your progress, about the next step, do you have any questions, this is why, how to do this, you know, getting them ready to take the next step.

It works. (Laughs.) About 420 books now. It works.

**Tammy Barley:** Ann, is there anything else you would like to add? Please feel free to.

**Ann McIndoo:** You know, the most important thing, I think, to getting your book done is wanting it. Really wanting it.

I tell you, and I find this so surprising, that sometimes people call me and say, "I want to write a book about ___." And I say, "That's a great idea, let's talk about it." They sign up, they send me money, and then I never hear from them. It always surprises me that they took the steps but they never followed through. And so I follow up with e-mails and letters, like come on, let's finish! I've found that people say, "You know what? At the time, I really wanted to do it, and as long as your program doesn't expire, I'll come back to you when I'm ready." And you know, that's fine.

So what I like to say is, when you start to write a book, really commit to it. Really want to do it. Because it's not a good feeling to start it and never finish. Like with anything else. That's why the three D's—be dedicated, determined, and disciplined—is really important. Really want it.

Then hire someone to help keep you accountable.

Also, have a porch date. That's something I made up.

It came about from this. Once my first book was submitted to the publisher, and the publisher told me my book would be here in about three or four weeks, I counted the days. Sure enough, one day this big, brown UPS truck drove up in front of my house. The guy opens up that big sliding door—I hear the roar of the door—and he pulls out his dolly. And there's three boxes, and they say *So, You Want to Write!*

Oh, tears were in my eyes! I've never been so excited! I lifted a fifty-pound box, and I opened it like a kid on Christmas. When I saw my book for the first time—I looked in the box, there they are, stacks of four all the way across. My beautiful books. Pristine, like little soldiers. I picked one up, and I held it. I was so excited, I started crying.

Then two things popped into my head. First, I did it. I am a published author. And the second thing was, Now, I have a tool. To show, to teach, to help others write their books.

And so, that day, I call my porch date. The day that the books landed on my porch.

So I always ask authors, when we first talk, in session number one, "So what's your porch date?" Lots of times they say, "Huh?" and I explain. Then I ask, "Will it be your birthday, or this Christmas, or do you want it for one of the holidays? The catalogues for the bookstores come out in September and April, would you like your book to be in there?" And I ask authors compelling questions.

And that's why I send them on that author's book tour. To imagine seeing their book in the store. When you do that author's book tour, and you go in the store, and lots of times I have them make up a mock cover of their book, even just taking a piece of printer paper, folding it in half, typing the name of their book, a picture, something, and then putting it on the shelf and taking a picture of it. When you walk out of that bookstore, you feel differently. You have taken on your author's identity. And now you are so excited to write a book.

And you have your porch date.

It's a really great way to get started, by having your vision and purpose, by having your porch date. And by having your discipline, your compelling future, and by being prepared. That's how your book's going to get done.

**Tammy Barley:** Ann, thank you so much for your time and your knowledge that you've so generously shared. It's been a great pleasure to have you with us.

**Ann McIndoo:** Aw, thank you. Thank you so much! You're very welcome! I'm delighted to be a part of your book.

## About Ann McIndoo

As CEO and founder of So, You Want to Write!, Ann will help you to get your book out of your head and a manuscript into your hands. Designed for professionals, entrepreneurs, business owners, coaches, and CEOs, Ann's coaching will guide you through a proven process and help you achieve your book-writing goals.

More about Ann:

- Published author, speaker, and ghostwriter
- More than 400 books produced, written, and published
- Creator of:
    - Writer's Power Tools™
    - Author's Coaching Program™
    - Manuscript Grid™
    - Author's Boot Camp™
    - Trigger Sentences™
    - Author's Retreat
- Author of *7 Easy Steps to Write Your Book!* (2012)
- Creator of *Author's Journal* (2012)
- Creator of the Author's Workbook—Updated for 2012

- Official Author's Coach for Steve Harrison's Quantum Leap Program (2010–2012)
- Author of Chapter 1 Essay in Justin Sachs' book, *Power of Persistence* (2011)
- Host and speaker at Speaking Empire (2010, 2011)
- Speaker at Six Figure Speaking Event
- Speaker at Mark Victor Hansen's Mega Book Event (2006–2010)
- Author of *So, You Want to Write!* (2007)
- Author of *Create Your Writer's Power Tools™: How to Write "On Demand"* (2006)
- Author of *From Blog to Book* (2005)
- Author of *Heartbeats in Paris* (a novel, 2012)
- Speaker, sponsor, and exhibitor at National Speaker Association (NSA) events (2005–2010)

**You can contact Ann McIndoo at:**

www.SoYouWantToWrite.com
(760) 771-8940

## A Quick Note to Readers

Each author's coach has a unique approach. If you choose to work with an author's coach, choose one whose strategies and methods you feel comfortable with, whose strategies and methods will work great for you.

I provide one-on-one coaching, as well as the 5-week business-book-development program Platinum Draft Webinar based on the content in *Business Gold*, both specifically designed for motivated business-book authors. To learn more, visit www.PlatinumDraft.com.

If, on the other hand, you're motivationally challenged, a coach like Ann who can help you get your head, bod, and environment into the game is a good way to go.

Ann has shared a number of phenomenal strategies to help stuck writers get your first draft onto paper or into your word processor. In the following chapters, I will show you more strategies to get your manuscript written, how to write to keep your readers glued, how to write the three different styles of books, edit to polish your manuscript to a golden finish, and a lot more, all designed to grip readers, get word-of-mouth referrals, convert readers into presold prospects for your business, and to drive them enthusiastically to your business door.

# Chapter 5

# Keep Your Readers Glued: The Top 5 Writing Techniques You Can Start Using Now!

Hold on to your seat—your writing abilities are about to accelerate. Here are the top five super-secret *fiction*-writing techniques you can use to grip your reader—and punch up the impact of your writing!—for every kind of writing you do.

## #1—Shorter Paragraphs

Just a glance at pages filled with long paragraphs can give the reader gloomy flashbacks to the stale, plodding textbooks he endured throughout high school and college. What's more, long paragraphs of justified text can be laborious for the eye to follow, and important points can be lost if buried among a dozen other sentences.

The fix is easy—shorten the paragraphs.

In fiction, authors use short paragraphs to speed up the reading pace and ratchet up the reader's interest, since short paragraphs quickly move his eye down the page and keep him turning pages quicker. It's the secret reason, unknown to audiences, why best-selling novels feel like, and are reviewed as, "page turners."

In nonfiction writing, this technique delivers a great bonus: Content written in short paragraphs impacts the reader strongest.

Think about it. Which information on the past few pages stands out most in your mind? Which is the easiest to recall? Exactly, the information presented in short paragraphs. Not coincidently, it is also the most important information.

Short paragraphs enable you to make one powerful, memorable point at a time. And they allow the reader to benefit from learning one concept at a time.

How can you develop this technique? Simple. Each mini-topic should have its own paragraph.

Try to limit most paragraphs to three or four sentences. If paragraphs are occasionally longer, no problem. You'll still keep your reader engaged, and the information will still stick in his mind.

Present the most important information in even shorter paragraphs, as short as one sentence, to ensure that content will stick.

A word of caution: Avoid too many short paragraphs in close proximity. Frequent use of short paragraphs will produce a staccato feel and draw the reader's attention to the technique and away from the information you want to provide.

## #2—Shorter Sentences

Shorter sentences deliver the same advantages shorter paragraphs do—the perception of faster pace, and solutions that stick. It's another super-secret fiction authors' technique.

Naturally, you want to vary sentence length and construction to maintain reader interest, but a sentence that goes on for six or seven lines will make your readers daft, because they'll lose the thread of thought that you started with, and become hopelessly mired among the tangents the concept takes, even though those winding tangents aren't too difficult to follow in spoken communication, since the ear can differentiate the pauses and shift in topics, whereas the eye of a reader becomes boggled with the lack of pauses especially if commas and other punctuation aren't frequently present to reveal those pauses and distinctions.

Make sense?

The basic rule—try to limit each of your sentences to a line or two.

The same word of caution as with short paragraphs: Avoid the distracting, staccato feel of too many short sentences in close proximity. You want the techniques to remain secret, invisible, so that they don't draw the reader's attention to them and away from your valuable content.

## #3—Back-Load Sentences

*Back-load?* you wonder. *Is that anything like the tractor?*

Actually, yes. It is. In fiction writing, the most important concept—the heaviest load, as it were—should be the last word in the sentence.

Why? Because the last word in a sentence is the most memorable, the one that resonates in readers' thoughts. That makes it the most powerful. So, when you write, place the most powerful word or concept last.

This will punch up that concept, and further help the information to stick in the minds of your readers.

The word or concept should not be a soft-sounding word, but one that gets noticed. For further explanation, see the next section, Use Words That Punch.

## #4—Use Words That Punch

As a reader, do you sometimes encounter text that's difficult to concentrate on? The reasons why are simple: The author:
- used long paragraphs
- used long sentences
- didn't back-load

- used soft-sounding words instead of words that impact

and/or

- used concept words with vague meanings

*Soft-sounding words* contain few of the hard-letter sounds that get noticed. **Here are the hard-letter sounds that do get noticed: long vowels and b, d, g, j, k, r, t, v, z.**

*Concept words* are those that the reader cannot visualize. They're vague rather than specific. A document packed with them is a challenge to concentrate on. The result? The prospect doesn't read much of the document, and he'll want to sidestep anything else produced by the same writer.

Worse is when vague concept words are positioned at the end of a sentence where the power word should go. Vague words are weak, and should be used to back-load only when you need to soften a point.

Here are examples of concept words that have vague meaning. Notice that most of these words are long with multiple syllables, and have soft-sounding letters like short vowel sounds and f, h, l, m, n, p, s:

| | |
|---|---|
| aspects | importance |
| achievement | improvements |
| approach | involvement |
| behavior | marketplace |
| commitment | organization |
| commonality | performance |
| competencies | principles |
| competition | progress |
| compliance | resources |
| effort | strategy |
| higher | unambiguous |

Two words to try to avoid: boring, ordinary. Using them will bore the reader.

Fiction authors manipulate word choice intentionally, in order to sound soft, strong, vague, warm, cold, and to deliver any of hundreds of other effects. You can easily apply this secret technique to your nonfiction writing, and keep your reader glued. And not just to your book.

If you've wondered why one or more of your white papers or magazine articles that you're working on isn't as effective as you would like, revise them with short sentences, short paragraphs, back-loading, and words with hard-letter sounds that define and impact.

## Thousand-Dollar Tip

A manuscript editor is the one professional—aside from a book-cover designer—that authors cannot do without. Select a top-notch editor who is also a multi-published fiction author. (I'll talk more about selecting editors later in the book.) Authors/editors employ scores of secret techniques to make your writing grip the reader, and are minute-detail gurus who can transform an ordinary manuscript into a superior quality book that will get raving referrals.

## #5—Delete the -ing

With -ing words (climb*ing*, approach*ing*), a few quickly become a lot. They soften words which weakens your impact. Also, –ings make words longer, which slows the reader's pace.

Whenever possible, fiction authors use the unchanged root verb (climb, approach) instead to avoid those effects—and to avoid the sound of too many –ings. An abundance of them echo in the reader's ear like a bell tolling; -ings distract and distance the reader from the points you want to make. Most often, the unchanged root verb (climb, approach) is more vivid, concrete, and has greater reader impact.

Delete the –ing to yield powerful words. Powerful words keep the reader engaged.

However, too many power words can cause the reader to feel talked at rather than conversed with. So, how many –ing words should you use? If possible, no more than one or two in each paragraph. When you focus on this strategy, your ear will start to pick out –ing-laden paragraphs as you reread what you've written.

This is not a point to be overly concerned about as you produce your first draft. For the first draft, simply follow the writer's axiom and write like you talk. Delete the –ings is simply a technique to keep in mind in order to bolster the effect of what you write. You can self-edit and rework the –ings later, after you complete the initial draft of your manuscript. For now, the goal is to compose the first draft with a few advantageous techniques in mind.

Shorter paragraphs, shorter sentences, back-loaded sentences, words with punch, and the reduced use of –ing words will become natural and easy to write with a little practice, and then all the documents you write will become stronger and more effective.

With those five techniques in mind, it's almost time to begin writing.

---

## Thousand-Dollar Tip

Research and fact-check for your book's main content after your first draft is complete (make quick notes for yourself as you go if needed). If while researching you come across information your readers would find helpful, you can easily add it to your manuscript. This way, you do not waste valuable time on "potentially useful" research that turns out to be a waste of time.

At the end of Part1, you chose your book style. Now we'll look at each of those three business-book styles with more detail in the following three chapters, one book style per chapter.

**Note:** You do not need to read all three of the chapters, and doing so may create confusion when you begin to write. Rather, I suggest that you read only the chapter that contains the information you need in order to produce your manuscript:

- Chapter 6 is for those of you who will write an informational/how-to book.
- To learn how to construct a biographical business book, read Chapter 7.
- If you will write an allegory, Chapter 8 is the place to be.

## Thousand-Dollar Tip

How many pages* should each chapter be? Plan for eight to twelve pages per chapter. Fewer is fine, but chapters consistently longer than twelve or fourteen pages may begin to feel laborious for your audience to read. If your book feels laborious to read, your audience will be less likely to recommend it or to be driven toward your business. Shorter is sweeter to your reader, and it also brings sweet rewards to you.

* "Page" does not mean *word-processor page* as you type it, but *book page* once it is published. Keep things simple. Set the page size on your word-processor document now to 6" x 9" with .75" margins, which will be approximately your book's final trim (book cover) size and margin width. You can adjust the trim size and margins later if you decide to use a different book size. I'll discuss options later in the book.

# Chapter 6

## Book Style:
## How to Write an
## Informational/How-To Book

### Informational/How To

- This is the most commonly used format for business books. *Business Gold* is the informational/how-to style of book.
- This structure works well for both B2B and B2C content.
- Information is clearly presented, in straightforward terms, enabling the reader to immediately apply the solutions.
- In addition to presenting information gleaned from personal experience and/or in-depth research, the author may use brief stories/parables (true or fictional), anecdotes, charts, graphs, illustrations, photographs, one-page cartoons, callout (text) boxes, and/or other graphics to convey data and its relevance, in any way the author chooses in order to achieve his goals for the book and reader.
- Informational/how-to books can be any length, but word count typically falls between 15K and 70K.

## Provide Great Information Fast

Due to the influence of the Internet, e-communication, demands on time, and our quick-paced culture, readers of informational/how-to books are conditioned to want great information fast. They want to get straight to the solutions they need.

To illustrate the point, I'll tell you a story.

While living in Michigan, my son, who was in seventh grade at the time, came home from school, and by the grim look on his face, I knew there was trouble.

Sure enough, an hour later, an angry father pounded on my door, his daughter, also in seventh grade, close behind him, sporting a couple of fresh stitches on her forehead. The girl, known to stretch the truth (and reinvent it, when convenient), had stirred up trouble in school before, and I'd already gotten the day's actual events from my son, whom I know to be honest.

Looking at her dad, I now had a pretty good idea where the girl had inherited her unreasonableness.

The man yelled, "Your son intentionally hit my daughter in the head with a tennis racket during gym class! I had to miss lunch to take her to the hospital for stitches, and if insurance doesn't cover it, you're going to pay the bill!"

I recalled a scene from a novel in which an attorney, when confronted with an angry crowd, calmly talked on and on (and on) until the crowd grew bored and finally dissipated. I was inspired with a means of handling the situation.

Showing concern to the girl, I fussed over her stitches, and asked her questions about getting the stitches, did they hurt, was it terribly difficult to go through the emergency-room process. She answered those simple questions honestly enough, so I started to ask her equally simple questions about what had happened during gym class.

"So you were playing tennis? Oh, badminton? Of course. And you were playing on the opposite side of the net from my son? Oh, the same side? Ah, I understand. So you were on the same team? No? I see, there were two badminton courts side by side, and you were playing on different teams. So, my son was facing you? No? I guess my son was basically beside you, then. He was in front of you, and not facing you?"

After about ten minutes of my cooing over her and showing great concern in finding out exactly how my thoughtless son had abused her (I knew he hadn't), the girl's dad began to shift his weight from foot to foot, looking a little less angry and mostly like he'd had a long day.

So I talked some more.

Another four or five minutes later, I'd actually gotten the truth out of the girl: She had been near the sideline shared by the two adjoining courts, several feet behind my son where he couldn't see her, and she had run forward into his racket when he swung back to hit his team's shuttlecock. She'd blundered, felt stupid, and so had blamed my son.

As the girl and I continued to chat about it, her dad stretched his back, looked around. Maybe envisioned a cold beer in one hand and a TV remote in the other.

Finally he interrupted me, and gruffly mentioned the hospital bill again. I kindly reminded him that the school had insurance for such things, so he need not worry on that account. Then, slanting a look toward my son and matching the man's initial sternness, I assured the girl's dad I would definitely deal with my son to the utmost degree that the situation required.

(I don't recall, but I probably got my son a dish of ice cream to calm his nerves.)

The point of the story is that unnecessary talk or writing will bore today's audiences. Readers want to get straight to the solutions you provide, so be sure not to dampen their enthusiasm with unnecessary content. Stick to your topics, or they'll start thinking about other tasks they need to do other than read your book or be nudged closer to your business.

In the following section are ideas that will enable you to do more than just convey information as you write. Here are great ways to Introduce, Inform, and Intrigue.

## Hook and Reel 'Em, Then Dangle New Bait—Introduce, Inform, Intrigue

To hook your reader, <u>introduce</u> (start) each chapter and section with a bang. A statement, statistic, fact, or brief anecdote that grabs attention. That introduces the problem the chapter or section will solve. That compels the reader to bite, hold on, and keep reading. Any or all of these.

The best way to get ideas is to page through your favorite how-to books and see how those authors hook you. How they introduce each section's information. Flip through *Business Gold* to review chapter and section introductions that particularly grabbed your interest.

Did the author make a statement? Ask a question? Dangle a morsel of information you were eager to know? Tug an emotion? Inspire a new idea?

As you read chapter and section introductions, make notes of the ones you like and why, and then use similar wording or setups for yours.

A great introductory sentence or two will inspire an author to write great content, and in turn will hook a reader's enthusiasm.

Once your reader is on the line (though it's cliché, I love a great fishing analogy), reel them down the page (<u>inform</u> them) by providing the answers they need, in whatever means will best connect with your specific audience and best reflect your distinctive brand.

For example, you might use the following:

- **Enthusiasm**—Be warm, positive, and enthusiastic to the degree that it matches the emotional tone of your audience and content.

- **Problem-solution format**—Describe one of your reader's aggravations, then show him how to break through that barrier.

- **Stories**—In church, when does the pastor's sermon hold your attention? When he tells a story. (After he delivers the point of the story, the listener's mind tends to wander toward other matters—the honey-do list, whether you turned off the coffeepot. . . .) We humans love a good story. Use a few brief stories to illustrate points and to make those points memorable. Try interesting case studies (customers' success stories). If you already use stories when speaking to your audience, use some of those.

- **Personal connection**—Connect with readers by inserting something tangible you and the readers have in common, such as coffee shops, classic cars, the scent of power tools that drives a man to fix something. Use personal stories to connect readers to you. Get them to take your side on page one through a personal experience of yours that they can relate to, then they'll gladly stick with you for a few pages, where you can personally connect with them again. Preface a story by telling the reader, in your own words, different each time, "I'm going to tell you a story." With this, they are instantly attentive to what follows.

- **Examples and analogies** with which your audience will identify. For men, football, baseball, sailing, and similar sports activities work great. For women, tennis, massages, sojourns to the spa, pilgrimages to Macy's. In books written for both genders, golf, downhill skiing, baseball, and fishing can hold their attention, as can driving and automobile references. For niche audiences, create examples and analogies particular to their interests.

- **Metaphors**—In their book *The Official Get Rich Guide to Information Marketing on the Internet*, authors Robert Skrob and Bob Regnerus use "The Five Kings of Internet Information Marketing" and a kingdom, wanderers, and a wilderness as ongoing metaphors to pictorially show readers how to develop and implement an effective online marketing campaign. Likewise, you can develop one or more metaphors for your book to make a concept easier to understand as well as memorable.

- **The five senses**—Let the reader see, hear, touch, smell, and taste on occasion (another fiction-writing secret). This adds great realism and makes each usage—and its related content— memorable. Have each description stand on its own, or use it as an analogy related to a concept you want to convey. Mention a curl of steam rising from a coffee mug. The click of high heels on a tile floor. A cinder block's weight or jagged edge. The aroma of charbroiled steak. The flavor of sweet and zesty barbecued ribs.

- **Q & As**—To keep the reader immersed in your content, occasionally ask questions. (You've noticed I engage you with occasional questions, yes?) Questions establish personal connections between the author and reader. They enable the reader to feel personally invested in, and part of, the book. That drives up their enthusiasm and their referrals, even if they can't quite put their finger on why the writing captivated them.

- **"The fact is . . ."**—"The fact is" is a subtly powerful phrase. Used sparingly, it captures readers' attention with each use (limit uses to four or five per book), and adds to your authority in their viewpoint. It's a fact.

- **Surprise sentences**—Depending on your brand, content, and audience, you might surprise your reader. Every page or so, phrase a sentence in a way that fascinates, delights, intrigues. Or concoct fresh analogies your reader can visualize or identify with. Those will stick in readers' minds, and they will repeat

71

the best ones to friends in conversation . . . who might ask where the analogy came from.

- **Quotes**—We humans also love intriguing quotes. Sprinkle a few into your manuscript. Be sure to credit the source—author, book title, publisher, copyright date, *or* URL, article title, publication date, author *or* speaker, place, occasion/event, date.

- **Occasional humor**—The top public speakers follow the proven standard that you need to make the audience laugh every three to seven minutes. It's the same with writing. Yes, even with writing a business book. Interject an unexpected dose of humor.

- **Bulleted or numbered lists** like this one for key points that you can state briefly. These create visual interest since they are different from standard blocks of text, and they also appeal to the reader simply because they deliver great information quickly. They reel the reader along.

- **Stepping-stones**—Here's an alternative to bulleted or numbered lists. When presenting a list of related information in sequential paragraphs, such as first step, second step, third step, clearly state the progression next to the step with definitive wording (First, you . . .). Make it easy for your reader to find and follow the information you present.

- **A list of helpful tips**—Tips are usually brief, quick to read, and easily applicable. For example: *10 Surprising—and Effective—Uses for Peanut Butter*, followed by a numbered list of ten applications of peanut butter. (Gets gum off your shoe, for one.)

- **Headers**—Headers are section titles, like **Hook and Reel 'Em, Then Dangle New Bait—Introduce, Inform, Intrigue**. How important are section headers in an informational/how-to document or book? Well, let's say you spot an article online or in a magazine, titled "The 9 Biggest Mistakes Home Buyers

Make and How to Avoid Them." As a culture that wants great information fast, most of us would skim the article for those nine headers, which are usually printed larger than the text and in **bold** type. When skimming, if you don't see those nine mistakes spotlighted as section headers, you probably don't read the article. At all. On the other hand, if headers are included, and if the information noted in a header is new to you, then you read that particular point. Section headers help you to not waste valuable time.

- o People who write informational/how-to books need to remember that that's how many readers operate. Those readers sometimes skim, and if the header suggests its information is pertinent, then they read it. That said, if you write specifically for entrepreneurs, most entrepreneurs will read virtually every word. So when you calculate how many sections, and section headers, to include, consider your audience and how that audience reads.

- o Quick reminder: It's important to create chapter titles and section headers that are very descriptive and also grip the reader, to keep them reading, to keep them turning pages. Section headers and sub-section headers alert the reader to a new topic, and reveal exactly what that topic is.

- o How many headers should you use per page? Too few will leave long stretches of uninterrupted text, which, to a reader's perception, slows the pace of the book. Several on every page will interrupt the flow of concepts your reader needs to absorb. Aim for one or two per page.

- o Additional benefits of headers—Readers who want to locate certain information can easily do so. Also, if the reader hasn't picked up the book in hours or in days, he can quickly glance at the last section headers he read, and easily recall that information, then be able to continue forward.

- **Graphics**—Charts, graphs, illustrations, photographs, one-page cartoons, and callout (text) boxes add visual appeal, and they reinforce, or provide supplemental, content for the reader. The use of graphics will be discussed in detail in Part 4. For now, know that you can make creative use of them.

To sum up, as you write each section, keep the reader engaged, not just intellectually/logically, but also visually and creatively. Insert one or two of the above into each section, to inform, and to hook 'em and reel 'em along.

After you've hooked and reeled 'em through a section, you finally come to the end of your topic. Now it's time to dangle new bait. <u>Intrigue</u> your audience and keep them reading with a glimpse of the juicy tidbits coming up next.

In fiction writing, that is a secret technique known as an ending hook. Ever stay up till the early hours engrossed in a novel you "just can't put down"? The author hooked you at the end of each section, dangled new bait with the last sentence or paragraph. In nonfiction, subsequent headers nicely do that trick for you, but you can also write in a teaser of the information to come. Hook and Reel 'Em, Then Dangle New Bait—Introduce, Inform, Intrigue.

## Start Writing

As I pointed out in Chapter 2, you may already have a few hundred pages of notes in the form of seminar transcripts, white papers, blog posts, articles that you own the rights to, and the like, ready to be compiled into a book. If so, arrange the documents according to topics, then insert the information into your word-processor outline of topics and subtopics, until all the information has been inserted where you want it to be. If you think of new information to add while you're working, go ahead and add it.

If, on the other hand, you do not yet have written information ready to compile, then with your outline of topics and subtopics in front of you, pick the topic you want to delve into most, and keyboard (or talk into your MP3 recorder or voice-recognition software) everything you want to share with your reader about that topic. Do this for each topic and subtopic that you outlined, until you've conveyed all the information you want to include in your book. If you use an MP3 recorder, you can have the recordings transcribed.

In Chapter 3 I recommended transcribing your own digitally recorded *notes* as a means to generate more ideas and to avoid writer's block. If you digitally record (speak) your *manuscript*, definitely feel free to have the manuscript itself transcribed.

Introduce, inform, and intrigue the reader until you have discussed all your topics and subtopics, then you will have completed the first manuscript draft, and be well on your way to producing an informational/how-to book that is unputdownable.

Happy writing!

# Chapter 7

## Book Style: How to Write a Biographical Business Book

**Business Biography**

- This is less commonly used than the informational/how-to format. *Rich Dad, Poor Dad* and *Midas Touch* are business biographies.
- This structure can work for both B2B and B2C content.
- Information is clearly presented, in straightforward terms, based on and described via the author's personal experiences and that of his associates and mentors, enabling the reader to immediately apply the solutions.
- In addition to presenting information gleaned from personal experience, that of his associates and mentors, and/or in-depth research, the author may use brief stories/parables (true or fictional), anecdotes, charts, graphs, illustrations, photographs, one-page cartoons, callout (text) boxes, and/or other graphics to convey data and its relevance, in any way the author chooses in order to achieve his goals for the book and reader. Authors of biographies tend to make lesser use of these tools than do

authors of informational/how-to books. Instead, the primary focus of a biography is on the story itself and the solutions it provides.

- Biographies can be any length, but word count typically falls between 30K and 70K.

- A business biography is recommended if you are a celebrity or have an established audience of thousands and have highly in-demand information to convey.

- Because of the biography's unique characteristics and the level of expertise required to write it successfully, I encourage all who wish to choose business biography as their book style to gain editorial assistance from a manuscript editor/ghostwriter who possesses proven know-how with writing business biographies. I'll discuss working with a manuscript editor later in the book.

## The Focus

A business biography reveals key life and professional events, and wisdoms gleaned from these events, that led to the author's success. The author uses his story to teach the reader how to do the same.

Perhaps surprisingly, rather than focus exclusively on self, many top-selling biography authors focus on other people, those who mentored, taught, and inspired them with their own experiences and wisdoms gained. The authors spotlight those mentors' characters, their means of teaching and inspiring, interspersed with the know-how the author developed through his personal trials, failures, and successes.

If you're a fan of *Star Trek: The Next Generation*, you might have seen the episode "The Chase." In the episode, Captain Picard's (played by Patrick Stuart) former professor gifts him with a hollow ceramic statue, called the Kurlan *naiskos*. The statue is basically a head and dome-shaped bust, which sits on top a ceramic base shaped like a round pie pan. Inside the base, many similar, miniature humanoid statues sit nestled together, representing a community of individuals within. The ancient civilization of the statue's craftsman believed "each individual is a community of individuals," that "inside us are many voices," each inner person with its own view of the world.

For authors of business biographies, that's an excellent analogy of our mentors' contributions to who we are and what we've accomplished.

Yes, readers will be eager to learn how you achieved all that you have done. But authors of biographies avoid overusing the words *I*, *me*, and *my* and avoid writing solely about themselves. In addition to writing scenes that detail the challenges they've overcome, they share their mentors with the reader, and shine some of their limelight on those people.

The authors do not self-aggrandize. They teach the reader.

Even in a biography, the reader is the star.

## Plan

A business biography is a compilation of experiences and knowledge gained. A *compelling* business biography is also a personal account of one's driving need to realize a dream or goal, and the internal and external blockades one must break through in order to realize that dream or goal.

To be sure you will engross the reader in your story and subject matter, plan your manuscript with the help of the following best-seller novel-writing techniques.

### Goal, Motivation, Conflict

A **plot** is the series of events that make up a story.

Fiction authors use goal, motivation, conflict (GMC) to develop plots that grip and hold the reader's attention. **Goal** is what the main character must have, cannot continue to live without. **Motivation** is why he must have it, no matter what. **Conflicts** are the insurmountable challenges he must overcome to reach his goal.

In a business biography, the "character" is you, and the events and challenges are real—your actual experiences. The more you can weave elements of GMC into your business biography, the more you will engross your readers, benefit your readers, and the more they will praise your book to others.

## Layout Options

In biographies, content is often written in chronological order so that the reader can easily follow the chain of events. Authors of chronological biographies also use various creative devices. For example:

- A distinctive **present-day event/scene** can serve as bookends to begin and end the story.
- **Flashbacks** during the story add intrigue as well as explain choices the author made.

In Chapter 2, you listed and organized the topics you plan to include in your book. (Biographies do not necessarily include chapter or section titles, though they can, but if you created titles for your topics, they will at least serve to inspire the development of their content.) As I mentioned a moment ago, biographies are often chronologies. If you didn't list your topics in chronological order (the order in which you experienced them), then ask yourself whether the order will matter to your reader, based on your goals for the book. If the reader will understand your content perfectly without a chronology, simply follow the topical order you developed in Chapter 2.

If, instead, your reader and your goals for the book would benefit from a chronological or another ordering of topics, use that.

Whichever layout will work best for your manuscript, GMC will be a key asset.

**Putting It All Together**

Here's how to plan your manuscript using GMC.

Keep your order of topics near you for easy reference.

Books that use goal, motivation, conflict begin with a compelling emotional experience, usually a life event of significant upheaval (a sudden and drastic change from what used to be normal), a revelation, or a need. In a business biography, that significant upheaval, revelation, or need should pinpoint the start, or a new direction, of your career.

In other words, who or what launched you on this career path?

Here at the beginning of your book is where you reveal to the reader your goal and motivation. Your goal should be the career goal that the earlier version of you will spend the rest of the book trying to achieve. Or your goal could be the terrible situation you struggled to get away from via a new career direction, which led you to where you are today.

Your motivation is why the Earlier You was driven to achieve your goal.

Now, mentally identify the key event that launched you on your career path, the event of significant upheaval, revelation, or need, which you will share with your reader.

This key event will be positioned at or near the beginning of the book. (If you use a present-day scene to begin your book, then flash back to the past when the key event took place, then the key event will be positioned *near* the beginning of your book.)

You can reveal goal and motivation subtly or plainly, whichever works best for you. What you need to do here is get the reader on your side, right on page one. Get him to identify with Earlier You's situation and/or Earlier You's desire for more or better. Or get the reader to identify with your present-day situation on page one.

Next, decide which event (and which information) will end your story. Again, if you use a distinctive present-day scene as bookends to begin and end the story, this last flashback event will be placed before the final bookend.

The final event should depict the achievement of Earlier You's goal. It should also be emotionally significant to End-of-the-Book You and/or satisfying to the reader.

Additionally, it should be the conclusion or end result of the business-related subject matter you will include.

Once you have identified how you want the book to begin and end—with which events and with which information—it's time to storyboard (or outline) how you will reveal each topic or solution that will fill the pages between.

## Storyboard

The best way to plot your business biography in detail is to storyboard. Or you might prefer to use an outline.

The list of topics and solutions you want to convey to the reader should be close at hand.

**If you storyboard**, use a single numbered sheet of paper or word-processor page to plan each chapter. The page number will be the chapter number.

Each chapter will present one main topic and its related subtopics, and the life event(s) that took place in which you gleaned that information.

You may opt to use a few flashbacks during the story to add intrigue as well as explain choices Earlier You made. If so, make a note where you will insert the flashback in the storyboard.

**If you outline**, each Roman numeral line should be a main topic. For that topic, each subpoint should detail, in order, the life event(s) and subtopics you will reveal within that scene.

Each main topic and its related subtopics will be its own chapter.

You may opt to use a few flashbacks during the story to add intrigue as well as explain choices Earlier You made. If so, add a subpoint where you will position the flashback in the outline.

Do this to lay out the entire story, whether you use a chronological or a topic-subtopic approach.

Be sure to plan memorable scenes, each of which should have an emotional connection or trigger for the reader, even if subtly. Each scene should be fascinating. Compelling. Each should also be a component of your GMC structure.

Before you begin, here is another great tool to consider.

## Headers

Headers are section titles, like **Storyboard** and **Headers**, and subsection titles, like **Putting It All Together**. As I noted a few pages ago, biographies can include chapter and section titles or not. If you opt to use them, you can insert the chapter and section titles you created in Chapter 2, or you can reword them if needed. Either way, they should serve to inspire your content.

How important are section headers in a business biography?

Well, as a culture that prefers to find great information fast, most of us skim an online or print article, or other informational writings, for headers that reveal the article's main points. Those headers are usually printed larger than the text and in **bold** type. When skimming, if you don't see topics spotlighted as section headers, you might not read the article. On the other hand, if headers are included, and if the information noted in a header is new to you, then you will read that particular point.

Section headers help readers to not waste valuable time.

That said, most business biographies are filled with content the reader has not encountered before, or has encountered before, but not in the way a particular author presents it. Which means a reader will probably read a business biography from cover to cover. Also, business biographies are personal stories, which by nature create reader interest, if written well. Further, if you write specifically for entrepreneurs, most entrepreneurs will read virtually every word.

So, readers of business biographies are more likely to read every page than, say, readers of informational/how-to books that could contain some information the reader already knows and therefore might skip over.

What all this means is that headers are optional, but by including them, you will help your reader to clearly understand what they are about to read, and the headers will also reinforce the concepts you convey.

Headers provide other benefits as well. New readers who want to locate certain information can easily do so. Also, if the reader hasn't picked up the book in a few days, he can quickly glance at the last section headers he read, and easily recall that information, then be able to continue forward. They also help the reader later, after they've finished the book, when they want to go back and locate certain information again.

How many headers should you use per page? Too few will leave long stretches of uninterrupted text, which, to a reader's perception, slows the pace of the book. Several on every page will interrupt the flow of concepts your reader needs to absorb as well as the flow of the story itself. Aim for one section header every three or four pages, or as needed.

Do your storyboard or outline now. For every chapter, include a descriptive, intriguing title, and equally effective subtitles if you wish.

Now, set the storyboard or outline documents aside for a day or two. Sleep on it. Then come back to it with a fresh perspective and verify that the layout works brilliantly.

Revise if needed. Sleep on it again. The story layout should be complete before you begin writing.

Once the storyboarding or outline process is complete, you will finally be ready to write. And each day that you work, you will know exactly what you will write that day, and exactly what you will write next.

Before you begin to write, here are a few last ideas to help you brainstorm *how* to write what you'll write.

# 4 Fiction-Writing Techniques That Dazzle

In a business biography, the writing itself is crucial to the book's success. Here are four techniques, honed and plied by top fiction authors, that will ensure your writing captivates your audience. As you read the following, add your ideas about each to your storyboard or outline.

### Who/What/Where

At the beginning of each scene, be sure to ground the reader in the scene. That means let the reader know who the story people are in this segment, what they're doing, and where they are. Even if you do this subtly and with few words.

For example. If in your previous scene you wrote about designing a golf course in Florida, and your next scene takes place five years later, and spotlights your business partner designing an atrium in Chicago, you'll need to indicate those details at the beginning of the new scene.

Otherwise, the confusion from those unknowns—"Wait, weren't we just designing a golf course in Florida? Where on Earth are we now, and what's this about an atrium?"—will be floating around in the reader's mind, distracting him from the points you're trying to make.

Keep the reader informed, even about scene details.

## The Five Senses

Make occasional use of the five senses. Let the reader see, hear, feel, smell, and taste. This adds solid firsthand realism and makes scenes memorable. Mention a curl of steam rising from a coffee mug. The click of high heels on a tile floor. A cinder block's weight or jagged edge. The aroma of charbroiled steak. The taste of sweet and zesty barbecued ribs.

You might also want to include how story people feel about (or react to) what they see, hear, feel, smell, and taste. That adds powerful realism.

How often should you include these? As I said—occasionally. Just like steak sauce, a little goes a long way.

## Let the Reader See

This writing technique works best for biographies that are entertaining and read like stories, compared to those that focus primarily on business and only include brief life examples in order to illustrate a point.

For every new person or place you introduce, briefly let the reader see him, her, or it. It's the same as when you meet a new person or walk into a new place—you quickly make a few observations about a person's appearance, or a few observations about a place's appearance and objects that are present. Do the same in order to enable the reader to see and experience the new person or place.

The reader only needs a couple of well-chosen details about an individual's appearance and/or movements, then they'll fill in the picture with their own imagination. The same with a place. You need only get their imagination started.

## Dialogue Tags

Like the previous section, this writing technique works best for biographies that are entertaining and read like stories.

Dialogue tags are simply those words attached to a line of dialogue that reveal which person is speaking.

"Said [person's name]" with the verb ("said") before the individual's name, is rarely used in modern-day writing. Why? Because it's not how people naturally speak, and therefore it distracts the reader and pulls them out of the story. Instead, simply write "[person's name] said."

Example:

- Archaic use: "If you can dream it, you can do it," **said Walt Disney**. (*said Walt* sounds awkward, distracting the reader from the story and its subject matter)
- Modern use: "If you can dream it, you can do it," **Walt Disney said**. (*Walt said* sounds normal, allowing the dialogue tag to essentially disappear into the page, so that the reader continues to focus on the important content)

Also, keep dialogue tags simple. "Mike said," instead of "Mike responded," and "Ann asked" instead of "Ann inquired."

Used subtly and sparingly, these four fiction-writing techniques will dazzle readers, though they might not know why they're dazzled. They can inspire your readers to praise your book to their associates as a must-read.

## Start Writing

With those ideas to inspire you, it's time to begin.

Place your outline of topics and subtopics in front of you. Pick the topic or life event you want to delve into first, and keyboard (or talk into your MP3 recorder or voice-recognition software) everything you want to share with your reader about that topic or event. Do this for each topic and subtopic that you storyboarded or outlined, until you have conveyed all the information you want to include in your book. If you use a digital recorder, you can have the recordings transcribed.

In Chapter 3 I recommended transcribing your own MP3-recorded *notes* as a means to generate more ideas and to avoid writer's block. If you digitally record (speak) your *manuscript*, definitely feel free to have the manuscript itself transcribed.

Once you have discussed all your topics, subtopics, and related events, and sprinkled it with a few top-selling fiction techniques, then you will have completed the first manuscript draft, and be well on your way to producing a business biography that is unputdownable.

Happy writing!

## Chapter 8

# Book Style:
# How to Write an Allegory

**Allegory**

- This is a less common, but often popular, format used to deliver individual or a few select business concepts. Thus, allegories are typically much shorter than other business-book styles. *Who Moved My Cheese?* and *The One Minute Manager* are allegories. An allegory is a fictional story that uses symbolic fictional characters (often not human) and objects to convey truths in order to benefit the reader.

- This structure works well for both B2B and B2C content.

- Information is creatively presented, in pictorial terms, to lead readers to useful conclusions.

- In addition to presenting information within a creative, fictional story, authors of allegories often make use of one-page cartoons and similar illustrations in order to achieve their goals for the book and reader.

- Allegories are commonly less than 20K words in length.

- Because of the allegory's unique characteristics and the high level of expertise required to write it successfully, I strongly encourage all who wish to choose allegory as their book style to gain editorial assistance from a manuscript editor/ghostwriter who possesses proven fictional and allegorical know-how. I'll discuss working with a manuscript editor later in the book.

## Plan

For centuries, world literature has been richened by symbolic fiction—allegories. John Bunyan's *The Pilgrim's Progress* and George Orwell's *Animal Farm* are allegories. In recent years, brilliant business professionals have used allegories, also called parables, to creatively convey information and new ideas to their readers.

Why do some authors choose to deliver their ideas via an allegory, as opposed to another book format? Several reasons.

1. **Size/word count**—Typically, an allegory presents one main topic and a few related subtopics—not enough content to fill a 50-70K-word informational/how-to book.

2. **A disarming quality**—Many allegories present ideas for behavioral change, often to audiences resistant to change. Allegorical stories are disarming due to fictionally entertaining plots, intriguing settings, and nonhuman or fictitious human characters who demonstrate, learn, and/or benefit from the experiences authors portray. With an allegory, readers can watch the story unfold from a relaxed and comfortable distance, like an audience in a movie theater. Readers' mistakes or disadvantageous paths are never directly addressed; the fictional characters' are, often by association of seemingly unrelated objects and/or events.

Thus, the disarming quality of an allegory opens readers to greater self-awareness and the solutions the story provides. Further, this book style often inspires readers with a vision of what could be, and influences them to achieve that vision.

3. **Creatively appealing**—Most potential readers know, on some level, that an allegory will encourage them to adopt a new behavior, to change. Some readers are more open to change than others. For readers less open to change, the actual story presented in an allegory is so creative and appealing that they want to read the story for its entertainment value as much as for its practical content.

4. **Memorable**—Due to an allegory's creative appeal, the story, if well planned and well written, will create vivid imagery and situations that linger in the readers' thoughts. When carefully planned and crafted, allegories can deliver significant personal and/or professional benefits to the reader, and because of this, the books often enjoy scads of reader recommendations.

5. **Illustrations**—Many authors add expertly crafted one-frame cartoons or cartoon-like illustrations to their allegories. These illustrations augment the books' key concepts. They also bring a fun, lighthearted feel to the pages, which further disarms and engages the readers, and makes the book memorable.

As you can see, meticulous planning before you write is key to producing an allegory of exceptional caliber.

So let's start planning.

In Chapter 2, you listed and organized the topics you plan to include in your allegory. Allegories do not necessarily include chapter or section titles (short allegories might not even include chapter divisions at all), but if you created titles for your topics, they will now serve to inspire the development of their content.

As you plan, keep in mind your audience, brand, and goals (mission statement) for your book. Write down or MP3-record every idea as it comes to you.

**The Story's Plot**

A plot is the series of events that make up a story.

Time to rev up the right brain, the creativity center. With your book title and main topic in front of you, brainstorm a fictional way to convey that topic . . . or, to disguise that topic. What story might you tell? What parallels can you draw on? What metaphors (likenesses or analogies) could you use? How might your message appeal to your reader? Free yourself to think of events and scenarios that seem either somewhat or completely unrelated to your topic.

*Who Moved My Cheese?* is an allegory that inspires humans to change when circumstances change, instead of ignoring or resisting change. The authors compare this human life concept to nonhuman characters who are in a maze, two of whom pay attention when circumstances change (which is to their advantage), and two of whom don't (to their detriment).

The maze symbolizes life. The cheese symbolizes one's primary goal in life (or in business).

*The One Minute Manager* is also an allegory. However, rather than employ symbology, the authors simply fictionalize human characters in realistic places and situations.

Which should you do? Your choice entirely. While you decide, consider that the more direct and personal to the reader that the nonfiction subject matter is, the more that reader will appreciate a greater degree of fiction.

In the book *Whale Done!: The Power of Positive Relationships*, mega-best-selling business author Ken Blanchard highlights the techniques Sea World orca trainers use to train five-ton whales . . . as a means ordinary people can use to inspire their fellow humans to perform better. Most readers are not resistant to this subject matter, so the story does not need to be extensively fictionalized.

Authors of the allegory *Fish! A Remarkable Way to Boost Morale and Improve Results* created a fictional manager in Seattle whose office is across the street from the real Pike Place Fish Market. In the story, the manager is tasked to turn an unenthusiastic team into a highly effective one. She draws on simple yet ingenious wisdoms she gleans from upbeat Pike Place fishmongers. That is the plot. Since many readers find themselves in the same situation as the fictional manager and are hungry for the answers the book provides, the authors did not need to fictionalize the characters or develop a lot of subtle analogies.

What change do you need to effect with your book? A mental change? An emotional one? Physical? How can you best represent the need for, and the eventual effect of, that change?

Think up dilemmas the character(s) will face, battles they must fight, answers they must find.

Fiction authors use goal, motivation, conflict (GMC) to develop gripping plots. These basic techniques will help you to develop yours.

**Goal** is what the main character must have, cannot continue to live without. **Motivation** is why he must have it, no matter what. **Conflicts** are the insurmountable challenges he must overcome to reach his goal. The more you can weave elements of GMC into your story, the more you will engross your readers.

Plan memorable scenes in which you will move the characters (and reader) away from unproductive behaviors and toward productive ones. Each scene should advance the concept, character, and reader one or two steps closer to the point of your story. Each scene should have an emotional connection or trigger for the reader.

If you need ideas and inspiration for your manuscript, reading several business allegories will provide it. You will find that in each, the premise is surprisingly simple. And also fascinating. Compelling. Many of these stories are page-turners. Often due to GMC and emotional triggers.

## Characters

As you've seen, characters in an allegory can be either human or nonhuman, like the mice in *Who Moved My Cheese?*. Again, the more direct and personal to the reader the nonfiction subject matter is, the more that reader will appreciate a greater degree of fiction—and perhaps even nonhuman characters.

You might have one, principle protagonist, such as the nameless "bright young man" who searched for a good manager in *The One Minute Manager*, or multiple characters. Sniff, Scurry, Hem, and Haw are the four who run through life's maze in *Who Moved My Cheese?*. Create one or two dynamic characters the reader will identify with and cheer for.

Create one or more dynamic secondary characters with goals or ideals that differ from or oppose those of the protagonist(s).

Use the characters to demolish old behaviors and build new ones, the characters' and the readers'.

Limit the number of characters to only as many as you need to convey your topic(s). Too many characters or unnecessary characters will muddy the story and confuse the reader.

As I pointed out, not all characters in allegories have names. Those who do are often named to represent a concept, quality, worldview, type of person, moral standard, or other trait, like Hem and Haw, or Christian, Obstinate, and Pliable in *The Pilgrim's Progress*. Choose clear, simple designations, keeping in mind that characters and their names are part of the subtext the author uses to inspire the reader to adopt a new behavior.

Whether the characters represent positive traits or negative, their names and personas should be chosen to keep the reader open to and engaged in the subject matter of the story. A name or persona may be negative in connotation, but it should also amuse on some level, even if wryly.

## Setting

A maze. A fish market. Sea World. A farm peopled with talking animals. Whether realistic or fictional, a well-chosen setting adds imaginative interest to the book. It also typically represents an important concept that meshes with the plot and characters to deliver the main point of the story.

A setting can be any place. It can be as small as a maze or as large as a continent.

It should be unique and memorable.

Think about settings in fictional stories you've read, or in movies you've enjoyed. Which settings are your favorite or have become popular? Why? Consider your answers while you plan your story's setting.

## Objects

Symbology, metaphor, added meaning beyond the obvious. Objects in allegories are carefully chosen to express subtle yet specific meaning to the reader.

Cheese can symbolize a goal. In the *New York Times* #1 best-seller *How Full Is Your Bucket?*, a dipper and bucket are the objects, the metaphors.

Symbols should be familiar objects the reader can mentally visualize, with three dimensions and full color. They should also evoke feelings for the reader, primarily positive. (Who doesn't love tasty cheese or the orca show at Sea World?)

## Narrator and Emotional Tone of the Story

You've likely sat around a campfire with family or friends on a warm summer night, and been captivated by someone who spun a good yarn. Perhaps you're a natural storyteller yourself.

In an allegory, you, the author, are the narrator. The storyteller. You reveal the story's events, one by one, to the reader. You describe the characters' traits, supply their thoughts. Tell the reader about the setting and the objects.

You also provide the emotional tone the story is told in— lighthearted, funny, adventurous, enthusiastic, thoughtful, or another emotional tone. Choose an emotional tone to reflect your brand and audience as well as your nonfiction subject matter.

Achieve that tone through:

- paragraph and sentence length (shorter for a lighter, more positive tone; longer for a more thoughtful tone)
- word choice (softness or hardness of letter sounds)
- the setting, conflicts, and objects you include in your story

## Storyboard

The best way to plot your allegory is to storyboard. Or you might prefer to use an outline.

List all your ideas for plot, setting, characters, and objects. Keep brainstorming new ones, until each element perfectly achieves every one of your objectives. Take as many days as you need. If you don't have brilliant elements, you won't produce a brilliant book.

Once you have chosen your elements, plan the precise order in which you will present all elements and topics. If you storyboard, plan scene by scene what will take place and be revealed—one scene per word-processor page.

If you outline, each main point should be a scene. Each subpoint should detail, in order, the elements and topics you will reveal within that scene.

Do this to lay out the entire story.

Note that modern allegories typically do not have chapter divisions.

Then, set the storyboard or outline documents aside for a few days. Sleep on it. Then come back to it with a fresh perspective and verify that the layout is perfect.

Revise for as long as you need to. Sleep on it again. The story layout must be flawless before you begin writing.

Once the storyboarding or outline process is complete, you will finally be ready to write. And each day that you work, you will know exactly what you will write that day, and exactly what you will write next.

# Headers

Headers are section titles, like **Storyboard** and **Headers**, and subsection titles, like **Narrator** and **Emotional Tone of the Story**. Allegories do not necessarily include chapter or section titles. However, you certainly can use them if you wish. By including them, you will help your reader to clearly understand what they are about to read, and the headers will also reinforce the concepts you convey.

Headers provide other benefits as well. If the reader hasn't picked up the book in a few days, he can quickly glance at the last section headers he read, and easily recall that information, then be able to continue forward. They also help the reader later, after the reader has finished the book, when he wants to go back and locate certain information again.

Quick reminder: It's important to create section headers that are very descriptive and also grip the reader's interest.

How many headers should you use per page? Too few might leave long stretches of uninterrupted text, which, to a reader's perception, can slow the pace of the book. Several on every page will interrupt the flow of concepts your reader needs to absorb as well as the flow of the story itself. Aim for one section header every three or four pages, or as needed.

The chapter and section titles you created in Chapter 2, you may wish to use now as chapter and/or section headers. Again, headers are optional. Use them only if they will benefit the reader.

Before you begin to write, here are a few last ideas to help you brainstorm *how* to write what you'll write.

# 4 Fiction-Writing Techniques That Dazzle

In an allegory, the writing itself is critical to the book's success. Here are four techniques, honed and plied by top fiction authors, that will ensure your writing dazzles your audience. Weave them into your storyboard or outline.

### Who/What/Where

At the beginning of each scene, be sure to ground the reader in the scene. That means let the reader know who the characters are in this segment, what they're doing, and where they are.

For example, in one scene you might show a young penguin, fluttering his wings atop an icy precipice, getting ready to leap into the sea for the first time. In the next scene, he might be several months older, and an expert swimmer, exploring beneath the Southern Ocean.

You need to show character, time, and place changes from scene to scene. Otherwise, the confusion from those unknowns—"Wait, wasn't he just a newborn ball of fluff? What's he doing swimming?"—will be floating around in the reader's mind, distracting them from the story.

Keep the reader informed and captivated.

### The Five Senses

Make good use of the five senses. Let the reader see, hear, feel, smell, and taste occasionally. This adds great realism and makes each scene memorable. Mention a curl of steam rising from a coffee mug. The click of high heels on a tile floor. A cinder block's weight or jagged edge. The aroma of charbroiled steak. The taste of sweet and zesty barbecued ribs.

Also be sure to include, even if briefly, how the character feels about (or how the character reacts to) what they see, hear, feel, smell, and taste. That adds even greater realism.

## Let the Reader See

For every new person or place you introduce, briefly let the reader see him, her, or it. It's the same as when you meet a new person or walk into a new place—you quickly make a few observations about a person's appearance, or a few observations about a place's appearance and objects that are present. Do the same in order to enable the reader to see and experience the new person or place.

The reader only needs a couple of well-chosen details about a character's appearance and/or movements, then they'll fill in the picture with their own imagination. The same with a place. You need only get their imagination started.

## Dialogue Tags

Dialogue tags are simply those words attached to a line of dialogue that reveal which character is speaking.

"Said [person's name]" with the verb ("said") before the individual's name, is rarely used in modern-day writing. Why? Because it's not how people naturally speak, and therefore it distracts the reader and pulls them out of the story. Instead, simply write "[person's name] said."

Example:

- Archaic use: "If you can dream it, you can do it," **said Walt Disney**. (*said Walt* sounds awkward, distracting the reader from the story and its subject matter)

- Modern use: "If you can dream it, you can do it," **Walt Disney said**. (*Walt said* sounds normal, allowing the dialogue tag to essentially disappear into the page, so that the reader continues to focus on the important content)

Also, keep dialogue tags simple. "Mike said," instead of "Mike responded," and "Ann asked" instead of "Ann inquired."

Used subtly and sparingly, these four fiction-writing techniques will dazzle readers—though they might not know why they're dazzled—and go a long way toward making your scenes unforgettable.

That inspires your audience to praise your book to their associates as a must-read.

## Start Writing

Now that your storyboard or story outline is complete, and you're full of great ideas, it's time to write.

Start at the beginning of your storyboard or story outline (for an allegory, starting at the beginning usually works best) and write the first topic's scene(s), the beginning of the story. Continue writing topic by topic, scene by scene, until you have conveyed all the information and story elements that you want to include in your book.

This step will be the bulk of your work, so take all the time you need.

Once you have discussed all your topics, subtopics, and related events, and sprinkled it with a few top-selling fiction techniques, then you will have completed the first manuscript draft, and be well on your way to producing an allegory that is unputdownable.

Happy writing!

Part 3

# Edit:
# Polish to a Golden Finish

# Chapter 9

# Self-Edit to
# Spotlight Your Expertise

Welcome back! By now you have completed the first draft of your manuscript—congratulations!

If you MP3-recorded your manuscript and haven't had the recordings transcribed into an electronic version, do so now.

You may have heard the writers' adage "Writing is rewriting." Just as you, as an entrepreneur, wouldn't sell an inferior product—in large part because of the way it would reflect on your business and current and future profits—neither would you choose to produce an inferior book, for the same reason.

Rewriting, also called self-editing, is essential to ensure that your book strikes gold. Electrifies your reader. Gets recommended. Drives presold prospects to your business.

How do you begin? By sleeping on it, if you haven't yet. Take a few days off. Set all thoughts of your manuscript aside. Then, with a fresh perspective, you will be ready to begin.

## Research and Fact-Check

Now is the time to research and fact-check. Fill in any missing pieces, double-check that facts and quotes are accurately worded and attributed.

To attribute, simply include, after the fact or quote: "Source: [author, title, publication details, date]" or, if from a spoken source, "Source: [person, date, occasion/event]." If in doubt whether a spoken source would want their quote used, gain written permission. If the quote is a small quantity of material, you may opt to paraphrase. Either way, attribute the source.

Rather than attribute the source in the text, you may prefer to include the attribution in a footnote, but consider that footnotes tend to add a scholarly feel to a book, and can distract the reader from the book's content. Unless attributions are frequent, I suggest adding the attribution into the text immediately following the fact or quote. However, if your book must contain multiple footnotes, then include the attributions there. Note that if you plan to e-publish your book, e-publishing platforms do not currently allow for the use of footnotes.

A word about the legal doctrine of fair use. Fair use "allows authors to quote from other authors' work . . . for purposes of review or criticism or to illustrate or buttress their own points. Authors invoking fair use should transcribe accurately and give credit to their sources." (Source: *The Chicago Manual of Style*, 15th edition (Chicago: University of Chicago Press, 2003).) So you can quote from another source, but again, be sure to attribute the source.

Do your research and fact-checking now. Insert any additions into your manuscript.

## Read through the Manuscript

Next, read through your manuscript draft. Verify that your information is complete. Verify that your topics and subtopics are well organized, in a logical progression, that each point is discussed completely, and only once. Make note of any topic that has been discussed in part or in whole more than once. You may find it helpful to write down a new list of the topics as you read, or to match them against your original list. Combine each disjoined topic in one place.

Confirm: relatively short paragraphs, short sentences, back-loading, words that punch, and that you've reworded to avoid a surplus of –ings. (Here's how to easily see the number of –ings. Use your word processor's Search and Replace function—search for "ing" and replace with bright green or aqua highlighted "ing.")

Make any updates to the writing as you read.

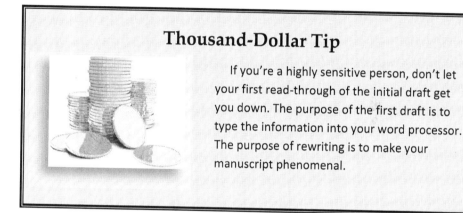

## Thousand-Dollar Tip

If you're a highly sensitive person, don't let your first read-through of the initial draft get you down. The purpose of the first draft is to type the information into your word processor. The purpose of rewriting is to make your manuscript phenomenal.

## Read through the Readers' Eyes

Now read through the manuscript again. Not as the author, but as a reader.

Out loud. Either yourself, or have your voice recognition software read your manuscript to you.

Is your writing warm and conversational? Or drier than a lizard's cough? You are not producing a dry college textbook, but an information-rich invitation to frequent your business. While rewriting, make sure you sound as if you're speaking with a prospect—relaxed and personable, while maintaining your target goals and brand.

"Professional" writing is not personable writing. Stiff, formal people are not comfortable to be around. People who are relaxed and genuine are.

In short—be yourself. You don't want to sound like every other writer. In fact, you don't want to sound like *any* other writer. Your writing should be memorable. Unique.

If you want to be certain you appear professional, slip in a three-syllable word now and then that makes you sound like the intellectual giant you are. Like Dijon mustard on a toasty BLT, a little goes a long way.

Maintain tight writing so that you keep the pace moving and the reader engaged. Don't use five words when you can use one.

Do you provide examples, analogies, and stories that match your brand and your mission statement for the book, and which your target reader can identify with? (< Yes, you can even place a preposition at the end of the sentence, if it enables you to sound natural.)

If you use contractions when you talk, then use contractions when you write. For example: I'm, you'll, isn't. (Though note: Do split contractions into the complete, original words to emphasize a point. For example, instead of *"Don't* feed the bears," *"Do not* feed the bears" delivers greater impact.)

Ask yourself reader-oriented questions as you edit: What is my reader thinking or feeling as he reads this? What is his reaction to the wording of this sentence, statement, or paragraph?

Your writing should frequently produce a positive emotional response, even if the emotion is nothing other than "Wow!" about your content.

Make readers feel great. About your book. About the new ideas your book evokes. About you. If they love your book, they'll look forward to seeing what else you have or can do, whether it's more books, more products, or more solutions.

With every page, enable readers to brainstorm and get excited about new ideas that strike.

Do you sound dedicated to the reader's success? You should. That's what the reader is dedicated to.

Do your topics pinpoint your audience's biggest problems and resolve them in easy-to-implement ways? Ask yourself this question, and answer it, as a reader.

Be sure chapter titles and section headers grab reader attention as well as precisely fit the content of each section. Reword your chapter and section titles where needed to best reflect their content.

Avoid industry jargon, so that you don't alienate readers (business prospects) who are new to the industry.

If writing for an international audience, be sure to avoid using colloquialisms native to your country that readers from other countries might not understand.

Are you less of a do-it-yourselfer and more of a delegator? You can opt to send your manuscript to an experienced business-book editor/ghostwriter and have them edit for you. I'll discuss working with a manuscript editor shortly, in Chapter 14.

## 10 Tips to Spotlight Your Expertise

Your primary goal for your book is to pull readers toward your business. But how do you introduce information about your products or service without it sounding like a sales pitch?

It's easier than you might think.

Here are ten ways to subtly, smoothly, suavely lay out the red carpet to your door:

- **Back-cover bio**—Your headshot photograph and mini biography will appear on the back cover of your book—one of the very first aspects of a book that a potential reader sees. (Detailed book-cover copy how-to coming up, in Chapter 13.) You're an expert at what you do, so in your bio, briefly tell the reader what you do. Add your professional title, the name of your business, and your tagline, if you have space. Follow this with your Web site URL.

- **Testimonials**—Writers of the testimonials that are printed on your book cover and in the first pages of your book might mention your business for you. Specifically ask one or two of them to do so.

- **Foreword**—The professional who writes your foreword can mention your business for you. Simply ask him or her to include a few glowing, truthful remarks about it.

- **Anecdote**—About one-third the way through your manuscript, mention an aspect of your work or business, as it relates to a topic. Reveal it through an anecdote, a moment experienced by you or a client.

  For example, one of my clients (I do work as a private editor as well as a book consultant) often uses anecdotes in his books, sharing with his readers the early days of his career, when he managed a bicycle store and discovered that sending out monthly newsletters to the store's customers netted ten times the annual profit within two years. (Which is a true story; the book I'm referring to is *The Magic of Newsletter Marketing: The Secret to More Profits and Customers for Life* by marketing expert Jim Palmer, whom I interview in Chapter 23). Jim uses that personal story to show his readers how custom newsletters (one of his popular businesses) can boost their sales and their customer retention. Thus, he uses the bicycle shop/newsletter anecdote to begin drawing prospects toward his newsletter business funnel. Voilà. No sales pitch.

- **Anecdote #2 and #3**—Insert another anecdote or short story about two-thirds the way through your book, and again in one of the last chapters so that the reader has your business benefits resonating in his thoughts when he finishes the book.

- **Shameless plug**—If you, your brand, and your target readers are a down-to-earth bunch, tell them plainly about your business (again, at least one-third the way through your manuscript), and tell them with a dose of good humor that it IS a shameless plug (or similar wording). They will appreciate your honesty, and the humor as well as your business will linger in their minds.

- **Expertise**—You're an expert; your book itself is tangible proof of that. Proof that you have even more to offer. Simply by existing, it advertises you. That said, in the second half of the book, reveal the extent of your expertise to the reader. Use a story that engages and entertains. For example, tell them of an incident that happened while you were on stage giving a ___ (fill in the blank) seminar for five thousand people.

  Note: The incident you reveal should deliver a lesson that the reader can adopt and profit from. If that is your primary focus, that will be the reader's as well (instead of them thinking of your anecdote as self-aggrandizing), though they'll also note your expertise.

- **Expertise #2**—This tip will nab *two* ways for you to gain. Mention to readers, either in the **text** or via **callout boxes** (such as my Thousand-Dollar Tips boxes; callout box details in Chapter 15), another helpful product or service you specialize in that they feel they *must* have.

  One way you can do this is to provide pointers about how to choose a certain kind of expert to assist them, and then show yourself to be the ideal choice.

  It's your job to make them feel like they must have that helpful product or service, cannot adequately continue forward without it. You can also reveal that no one else provides the solution(s), if that is the case. Include your Web site URL each time you offer to provide additional information or another helpful service, so that readers can easily locate the information or assistance.

By doing so, you 1) spotlight this second area where you excel, which will propel many readers to your business and 2) emphasize that you excel in the first area.

- **Cross-promote**—Should you learn that a colleague is also writing a book and his target audience overlaps yours, cross-promote each other once or twice in your books. You might also consider writing the foreword or testimonials to help each other expand your prospect pools.

- **Bonus materials**—After the text of your book, in the back matter, include one or more bonus materials—valuable offers and discounts to your business that your readers will be eager to take advantage of. Now is not the time to be stingy; that would be like shooting yourself in the foot. Be willing to temporarily lower your profits to entice new customers over the threshold. Get them in the door.

- **About the Author page**—You'll hint at your business and expertise in your mini bio on the back cover. You can also add more detailed information in a longer bio at the end of your book, on an About the Author page. It contains the same information that you included in your back-cover bio, and also a lot more about you professionally.

How to write the About the Author page is detailed in Chapter 12.

From the above, choose the option(s) that work best for you as you self-edit. Mention your business two or three times, but not much more than that, or you'll risk sounding like a sales pitch. Work in just a few, memorable details about your business to entice readers to become customers or clients. Let readers know what else you do, and provide subtle yet compelling benefits to drive up the readers' eagerness to further invest in your business, to gain even more solutions.

Make readers *need* another one or two of your products or services. Subtly use your book to spotlight your business and to place it in demand.

## Refine to Achieve 24-Karat Gold

The designation 18k, 14k, or 10k means that the gold has been alloyed with another metal(s) to form the piece of jewelry or other item. The designation 24k means the item is pure gold. Pure gold comes about through detailed refining.

An exceptional manuscript that excites and presells prospects is achieved the same way.

Now that you have read through your manuscript and made updates, both as the author and as a reader, and have spotlighted your expertise, the manuscript is ready for a final self-edit. A final, detailed polish.

In this self-edit, the goal is to be sure you have written conversationally, but also with distinctiveness and authority, to position the writing quality itself above anything the competition could hope to produce. This is where you grab readers', reviewers', and bookstore buyers' attention with your skill with words, as well as with the advanced instruction you provide.

I didn't show you these techniques until now simply because they would have been a lot to concentrate on while you wrote the first draft. However, these techniques are relatively easy to update when you self-edit.

For each of the following, make several updates throughout your manuscript:

- Replace **adjective**-noun combinations with strong, vivid nouns. Instead of _very good_, say *exceptional, superb.*
- Replace **adverbs** with strong, vivid verbs (adverbs often end in –ly). Change *"speak slowly and distinctly"* to *"annunciate"*;

*"significantly increase"* to *"explode"*; *"quickly draw"* to *"sketch."*

- Need ideas for words to replace those adjectives and adverbs? A great, free location to find them is <u>www.Thesaurus.com</u>.

These simple changes will ratchet up the impact of your writing and tighten it, which means you'll use fewer words and thus increase the readers' perceived reading pace and interest.

More updates to consider:

- Creatively use **similes** to explain concepts. Similes compare two different items using the words *like*, *as*, or sometimes *than*. Example: Drier than a lizard's cough. Be original so that your personality (even if somewhat nutty or irreverent) stands out as unique. See next idea.

- Reword **clichés**. Clichés are trite phrases that get overused to the point that they no longer impact the audience, but instead are stale, unimpressive, and cause readers to mentally yawn: bold as brass, right as rain, in the nick of time, the time of my life, old as the hills, fit as a fiddle, scared out of one's wits, all is fair in love and war, the writing on the wall. . . . Get the picture?

    Instead, concoct original phrases, phrases that are so fantastic that readers repeat them (and perhaps reveal where they heard the phrase). While self-editing, each time you spot a cliché, invest several moments forging a catchy new phrase.

- Avoid the indefinite words **some** and **thing**. Using the Search and Replace option of your word processor, highlight in a vivid color all uses of *some* and *thing*. Reword as many as possible with accurate word choices.

    True story: Years ago when I worked in a department store, a woman in a hurry needed to find an item. She described this item with—I counted—five uses of the word *thing* in a single sentence. Then she was actually exasperated when I didn't understand what she was talking about. My point? Reword virtually all uses of *some* and *thing* so that your reader understands exactly what you mean.

- Avoid **alliteration**. Alliteration is the repetition of a word sound, usually an initial word sound, in close proximity: Harry hallucinated hiding his hat inside a hiccupping halibut. Often comical (even when unintended), alliteration draws the readers' attention to the sound and away from the subject matter.

- Avoid **word repetition**. We all have favorite words we like to use. Learn to spot pet words and phrases and to reword. As I noted earlier, a great, free place to find ideas is www.Thesaurus.com.

Also, writers often misuse, or overuse, punctuation when writing books. Remember, book writing is not copywriting.

- **Exclamation points** (!). Used sparingly, exclamation points can emphasize a word or concept. Too many of these produce the same numbing effect as clichés, and they lose all value as a tool.

- **Quotation marks** (" " and ' ').
  - Double quotation marks (" ") are often "wrongly" used. (<Used around the word *wrongly*, as if to emphasize the word, the double quotation marks actually mean *so-called*, which negates the content in quotation marks—the exact opposite of what the writer intends.) Correctly:
    - Use double quotation marks around a verbatim quote: "The successful man will profit from his mistakes and try again in a different way." (Dale Carnegie)

- Use to indicate a person or character's dialogue: "I'm here to rescue you," Luke Skywalker told Princess Leia.
  - o <u>Single quotation marks</u> (' ') indicate a quote within a quote: "Neil Armstrong said, 'One small step for (a) man, one giant leap for mankind,'" Walter Cronkite reported.
- **<u>Ellipsis points</u>** (. . . . and . . .).
  - o Use <u>four spaced dots</u> to indicate a trailing off at the end of a complete sentence. The first dot is actually the period: "If you can dream it, you can do it. . . ." (Walt Disney)
  - o Use <u>three spaced dots</u> to indicate missing text within a sentence: "Have the courage to follow your . . . intuition." (Steve Jobs)
  - o Or use <u>three spaced dots</u> to indicate a trailing off at the end of an incomplete sentence: "If only . . ."

Writers often misuse, or overuse, font effects:
- **<u>Italics</u>**. Like exclamation points, too many italics produce a numbing effect, and draw attention to the font itself.
- **<u>Bolded</u>** words. Use only to spotlight critical points, headers, and subheaders. Too many draw attention to the print on the page. Readers start to notice how you're writing instead of what you're writing.
- Words in **<u>all capitals</u>** used to emphasize. WORDS IN ALL CAPITALS MAKE BOOK READERS FEEL LIKE THEY'RE BEING SHOUTED AT.
- **<u>Underlined</u>** words. Try to use only to highlight key elements in a list, like I'm doing here.

A *combination* of the "above" is even **worse**! Using a **variety** of font *effects* in <u>abundance</u> can **DISTRACT** your *reader* from "what" YOU are trying to <u>**SAY**</u>!!! Font *effects* "push" readers **away** *and* **force** them to reread and work **harder** to <u>understand</u> "what" they are reading!

So, apply font effects sparingly when writing a book.

Instead, to emphasize key points, reword. Use shorter paragraphs, shorter sentences, back-loading, and strong letter sounds.

## Final Notes

All of the self-editing techniques I discussed in this chapter will help your manuscript to strike gold in the minds of your readers. However, you should not spend months, or even weeks, self-editing your manuscript. The goal is to jazz the reader and get a zillion referrals, not to win a writing award.

You need to finish the manuscript, publish it, and start profiting from it. That won't happen if you endlessly analyze and tweak it and never get it out of your word processor.

Take time to complete your rewrites (self-editing) now. If you don't have the time or inclination to self-edit to the extent you need, or if you can no longer read your manuscript from a fresh perspective, you can send your manuscript to an experienced business-book editor/ghostwriter and have them edit for you. I'll discuss working with a manuscript editor soon, in Chapter 14.

# Chapter 10

# Add Front-Matter Pages

We're on the finishing touches of your manuscript. Front matter is simply the pages that appear before the main text of the book. Front matter includes the Foreword, Preface, and Introduction pages.

If you read Chapter 6, you saw the following, but it is worth the repeat: Due to the influence of the Internet, e-communication, demands on time, and our quick-paced culture, readers want great information fast. Fewer and fewer readers invest the time to peruse a book's front matter. They want to get straight to the solutions they need.

When deciding which front matter to include, it's important to always keep the reader's viewpoint in mind. If an author includes pages and pages of front matter, a potential reader who flips through those pages at the bookstore or a seminar, eager to glimpse solutions, may be put off by what they see as unnecessary content. Worse, they might see the author as long-winded, and surmise that if the author can't get to the point here, it's unlikely he'll quickly get to any point once the chapters begin.

You have to sell the reader on every aspect of your book.

When deciding which front-matter pages to include, try to include only the pages that are necessary.

So, which sections should you include in the front matter of your book? Dedication page? Epigraph? Foreword? Preface? Introduction? All of them? One or two? Why or why not? What is the difference between the Foreword, Preface, and Introduction?

I'll answer those questions, show you what to include, how, and explain the benefits of including or excluding each section, in the order the sections typically appear in a book.

## Testimonial Pages

Include.

As the first pages of a book, testimonials are one of the chief selling points for a potential reader who picks up your book at a store or seminar, hears about it through your marketing campaign, or discovers it during an online search.

While he scans the opening pages, a potential reader is looking for motivations—in addition to those presented on the cover—to purchase, or not purchase, the book. If he doesn't find any testimonials, he assumes no one was willing to write one due to the manuscript's poor content.

No testimonials, no sale. To an undecided buyer, testimonials are proof that the author is known as an expert on his subject matter.

### What Makes a Testimonial Compelling?

A compelling testimonial will contain the following elements, in any order that enables it to hook and reel in the reader. It will:

- **present a mini story in a problem-solution structure that echoes the potential reader's problem and convinces him he has found the solution via the testimonial writers' experiences.** (*Problem:* "Our sales numbers had steadily declined, and we had been forced to cut expenses by shrinking our staff. Then we faced a dilemma: How do we achieve more with less? *Solution:* Immediately after I read [*Book Title*], we began to implement its strategies. Within two months, our sales numbers had grown 18 percent. . . .") The testimonials should erase any doubt that could remain in your potential readers' minds.

- **detail specific benefits to the reader.** (*"[Book Title]* taught me everything—and I mean everything—I needed to know about ___, from [detail], to [detail], to [detail].")
- **include statistics/metrics.** ("After only sixty days, my new-customer inquiries increased by 42 percent. . . .")
- **deliver realistic yet effervescent praise for the book and its author;** the greater and more credible the praise, the more compelled the potential reader will be to keep reading or buy the book. ("If *[Book Title]* had existed when I first started in business, it would have saved me ten years of learning at the School of Hard Knocks, and I would have achieved success a full decade sooner.")
- **overcome objections the prospective reader might have.** You need the prospect to read the book. If they don't read it, they won't be drawn toward your business. Be sure testimonials will relieve them of objections they might have so they are eager to purchase a copy.
- **contain, in its signature lines:** the testimonial writer's name, professional title, business name, business Web site URL, all usually flush right, to properly credit the source as well as to underscore the source's credibility:

—John Smith, Owner
Business Name
www.BusinessWebSite.com

or

—John Smith
Owner, Business Name
www.BusinessWebSite.com

## How Many Testimonials Should You Include?

Obviously, one hundred would be too many, and two would look bleak as a sputtering neon *Vacancy* sign along a desolate roadside.

Include four to five minimum, and fifteen to twenty maximum. Few people take the time to read more than a couple, so aim for four to eight. Good information fast.

## Organization

There is no "right" way to organize the testimonials you receive. Here are a few options.

**Organize by Impact:** Place the most impactful first, then the next most impactful, and so on, since the potential reader usually reads the first few then skims the rest. The most impactful testimonies contain the highest number of compelling elements, brilliantly written. They might also be the ones that simply wow you when you read them.

**Organize by Name or Brand Recognition:** If a particular testimonial writer's name or brand commands high respect in the eyes of your core audience, place it first. Place the next highest respected second, and so on. Most readers scan the names of the testimonial contributors, if not the testimonials themselves.

**Organize to Benefit Your Business:** If you want to give a particular testimonial writer special recognition that he would appreciate and possibly reciprocate, or if he will be a major buyer of your resources, then place his testimonial first. His testimony benefits your business, and your special recognition benefits his in return.

Choose one of these organizational options, or combine them. Or another ordering may prove more effective. Decide who needs to benefit from the testimonials, how, and why, then plan the order based on those goals.

Once your books are widely known and sought after, name and brand recognition will sell your subsequent books for you, and testimonial pages will no longer be as critical, though they will still hook new readers. Until then, definitely include testimonial pages to help you cinch the sales.

## Title Page

Always included.

It displays, from top to bottom:

- book title
- book subtitle (if any)
- author name
- "With a Foreword by [Eminent Person]" (optional, but recommended)
- the publishing company's name and location (city, state, country) (this may also be placed on the copyright page) *or* your business name if the book is self-published

After the book is published, the title page becomes a great space to personalize and autograph the book for fans and new readers.

## Copyright Page

Always included.

It displays, from top to bottom:

- the publishing company's name and location (city, state, country) (if not included on the bottom of the title page)
- copyright notice: the word Copyright, the symbol ©, the year that the book is published, then the copyright owner's name. For example: **Copyright © 2013 by [Your Name]**

The symbol © is needed for international copyright protection.

Remember that copyright does not protect ideas or facts. Instead, it protects the way those ideas or facts are specifically worded in published form. Another person can copy your *ideas*—that's what people do when they research. Another person cannot, however, copy your exact *words*. That is plagiarism.

- "All rights reserved."
- country the book is printed in, such as "Printed in the United States of America"
- ISBN (International Standard Book Number). The thirteen- or ten-digit ISBN identifies your specific book, which helps the ordering and tracking process go quickly and smoothly.

  The first digit reveals the language the book is published in. The following group of three digits identifies the book's publisher. The next group of numbers identifies the book itself. And the final digit is the "check digit," which mathematically reveals if an error exists in the book number that precedes it.

  ISBNs are assigned in the United States by the R. R. Bowker Company (www.MyIdentifiers.com). Typically, your publisher or self-publishing company obtains this number for you. If you are uncertain whether they provide this service, ask them. Have them get the ISBN in your name, not theirs. If they won't, get the ISBN yourself, in your name.

  Each edition and binding (for example, soft-cover, hardcover, downloadable, audiobook) of your book will have a different ISBN.

- acknowledgments, permissions, and other credits, such as acknowledgments of contributors and cover and interior artists
- Library of Congress Control Number (LCCN). You'll see this number on the copyright page of this book. If (and only if) you want to sell your book to libraries, then you will need to get an LCCN for your copyright page *before* you publish. Note that libraries choose which books they will stock. An LCCN does not guarantee libraries will carry your book. (To apply for an LCCN, you must become a "publisher"; see Chapter 23.)

For more information, or to apply for your LCCN, visit the Library of Congress at www.loc.gov/publish/pcn/. When the number is preassigned (assigned before publication), it's called a Preassigned Control Number (PCN). The Library of Congress does not charge for this number.

The process of applying for and obtaining a PCN or LCCN can take up to two to four weeks, though mine took one day.

Once your book publishes, the Library of Congress requires you to send one copy of the book to them.

- The copyright page should also display a DISCLAIMER AND/OR LEGAL NOTICES paragraph like the one on my copyright page. Here is another one, based on a declaration jointly adopted by the American Bar Association and the American Publishers Association:

  o No express or implied guarantees or warranties have been made or are made by the author or publisher regarding certain incomes, earnings, profits, or other financial claims. Individual results vary, in large part, due to individual initiative, activity, and capability, as well as varying local market conditions and other factors. Neither author nor publisher accepts any liability or responsibility to any person or entity with respect to any loss or damage alleged to have been caused, directly or indirectly, by the information, ideas, opinions, or other content in this book/manual/course. If you do not agree to these terms, you should immediately return this book/manual/course for a full refund.

- your Web site URL (optional)

## Dedication Page

You may opt to include it or not. It's entirely your choice. The words "Dedicated to" are not necessary. You can simply write "To Carl and Sarah," or "For my wife," or "In memory of my father, Victor Downey."

## Epigraph Page

You may opt to include an epigraph (quotation that suggests the book's content or theme) or not. It's entirely your choice. Either way, remember to keep the reader's perspective in mind.

The source of the epigraph usually follows on its own line.

For example:

> "Always acknowledge a fault.
> This will throw those in authority off their guard
> and give you an opportunity to commit more."
> —Mark Twain

## Table of Contents ("Contents")

Always included in informational/how-to books and most business biographies. Allegory authors often omit it.

The TOC lists all of a book's sections that follow it, but not the sections that precede it.

You may include just the unit titles (if any) and chapter titles, or you may also include each chapter's section titles to make specific information easy for the reader to find.

Keep the table as short as possible. Few potential readers want to wade through a TOC a dozen pages long. If possible, limit its length to one to three pages. Keep potential readers eager to see more.

If your book is three hundred pages or more, or has a lot of topics and subtopics, allow the TOC to be longer.

However long or short your TOC, format it so that it's very easy to read. (Here, the word *format* means how your text looks on the page.)

## List of Illustrations, List of Tables

Rarely included. Add a list of illustrations, or a list of tables, page only if your book contains multiple illustrations or tables that will be frequently referenced, or that the reader may wish to easily locate again.

## Foreword

Optional, but recommended.

Many authors misspell it as "forward," meaning "progressing ahead." The correct word, foreword, is a combination of "fore" as in be*fore*, and "word" as in, well, *word*. A foreword is information that comes be*fore* the main *word*s of a book.

A foreword is usually written by someone highly respected by the reader, but who is not the author. This endorsement can bolster your credibility and expand your customer base.

The eminent person writing it may spotlight the book's content, the quality of the book, the author's expertise, the author's business, and/or his or her own personal connection to the author.

It should underscore the reader's belief that he definitely has, in his hands, a resource that provides exactly the solutions he is seeking.

If one of your goals is to become more well known in a particular field, someone who is well known in that field is the one to ask for a foreword.

How short or long should the foreword be? One to two pages, no more than three. If a reader sees pages and pages of front matter, he might skip the front matter entirely, and miss important information he needs to know.

## Preface

Optional, but this is a page I usually recommend not including.

Written by the author, it usually reveals why he wrote the book, how he conducted his research, if relevant, and it may contain acknowledgments, which I recommend placing on its own page.

Also, the word *Preface* tends to feel negative to the reader, who sees the word and recalls the old days of high school and college, when textbooks' Prefaces dragged on for twenty pages yet contained little of value.

How short or long should a preface be? One to two pages.

Again, I recommend omitting it, if possible.

## Acknowledgments

Optional, but recommended.

To give you a few ideas, you could acknowledge, each group in its own paragraph, the following:

- Those who have influenced your business, career, or you personally
- Your customers or clients who no doubt inspired your book and who make your career a joy
- Your partners, team, and those who assisted you to create the outstanding book the reader sees before him
- Consultant, artist, editor
- Your spouse and family, if for no other reason, because of your prolonged absence while you wrote madly and burned up one keyboard after the next, at all hours

How long or short should the Acknowledgments be? If possible, less than one page. If it takes more than a page, no worries. These people deserve the gratitude.

Here's how to format it. For brief acknowledgments, such as a few phrases, center between left and right margins. For longer acknowledgments, use paragraph form with indents.

## Introduction

You may opt to include it or not. It's your choice.

That said, this information written by the author about the book's subject matter is often helpful to the reader in understanding key concepts about what they are about to read, how the information is organized or presented, or how the reader is going to benefit from reading the book. Or all three.

The word *Introduction*, like the word *Preface*, tends to feel negative to the reader, and prompts the same high school and college flashbacks to those endless Introductions that contained little value. Solution? If you need to include several pages of front matter, I recommend titling this section A Letter to the Reader, which transforms the old staid, stagnant title for one that is fresh and personal.

Again, try to keep it to a page or two, as brief as possible, so that the reader's excitement for the book's information isn't weighed down with talking and talking . . . and talking.

So what should you include in the Introduction, aka A Letter to the Reader?

Well, you know readers' favorite radio station, yes? It's WII-FM— What's In It For Me? Tell them the best highlights of what your book will do for them.

Also, make it exciting! Your reader is thrilled to finally find your book—they've been looking for a book like it for years—and they want that excitement to continue. So continue it. Be thrilled to give the reader solutions! This is where you excel and what you love. Let your enthusiasm shine in the Introduction, as in the rest of your book.

If most of your readers don't know you—and if your goal for the book is to gain new prospects, most readers will not know you—then introduce yourself to your readers. Briefly tell them your unique story: How, and how long ago, you came to be in this business, why you're qualified to share what you know.

Include these—WII-FM, excitement, and your story—in any order that will captivate your reader and compel him to keep reading.

Follow it with your signature, if possible. Again, this is more personal than simply typing your name.

After the Introduction, your chapters and main text—the heart of the book—begin.

## Write the Front Matter

Write and add your front-matter pages now, with the exception of the testimonial pages and foreword.

Next, convert your manuscript document to PDF, then contact colleagues to request testimonials, and connect with the person who you wish to write your foreword. As people agree, send them your book summary (the back cover copy) and the PDF.

Once you receive the testimonials and foreword, add them to your manuscript document.

Your writing work is almost finished. There are only a few content ideas left to consider.

# Chapter 11

## Chapter Summaries

Chapter summaries—placed at the end of each chapter—are a great way for the reader to review the highlights of the chapter they just read. Since key points are restated, the summaries help to make those points stick.

Thus, the reader retains book details better. This delivers added value to the reader.

Also, if a reader finishes a book and weeks later wants to review certain information, end-of-chapter summaries (along with a descriptive table of contents), makes the information easy to find.

Too, the summaries can be action steps that the reader should take to achieve his particular goals.

That said, chapter summaries are, of course, optional.

End-of-chapter summaries typically appear on a single page, but can be longer.

These summaries work well for informational/how-to books, and authors of business biographies often add summaries or action steps. Allegories tend not to include page-long summaries, but their authors can insert, after each main topic and its related subtopics, a few notes or an illustration that underscores essential concepts.

If your informational/how-to book is fairly short—30K words or fewer—you might not have enough information in each chapter to need chapter summaries. Instead you may opt to include, in the back matter, an end-of-book summary, a two- or three-page compilation of the main points of the book, listed in order by chapter. (In Chapter 12 I'll show you an example of an end-of-the-book summary.)

On the other hand, if your informational/how-to book is fairly long—70K words or more—any chapter summary would be extensive as well. Your chapter just went on for pages; your reader doesn't want the replay to go on for pages too. If that is the case, in lieu of summaries, include a handy index in the back of your book, so that important information is easy to find.

So, if your book's word count falls between 30K and 70K words, give or take, end-of-chapter summaries might work great for your readers and your goals for the book.

How do you cobble together a chapter summary? It's easy. You or your manuscript editor can simply pick out the key points of each chapter, and place them in a bulleted list on the page immediately following the last page of the chapter.

Bulleted lists do not need to include bullet graphics. Feel free to use any graphic, custom or otherwise, that fits with your reader and your brand.

In her book *7 Easy Steps to Write Your Book: How to Get Your Book Out of Your Head and a Manuscript In Your Hands!*, Ann McIndoo used stars in the place of bullets.

In Jim Palmer's book *Stick Like Glue: How to Create an Everlasting Bond with Your Customers so They Spend More, Stay Longer, and Refer More!*, in which glue provided subtle imagery throughout the book, the "bullet points" were miniature sticky notes, and the summaries were cleverly titled "Sticking Points."

For example, if *Business Gold* were shorter, I might have included end-of-chapter summaries, maybe titled Golden Nuggets, and featured small gold bars as bullet points, to subtly represent the solidarity and value of each concept. A summary for the previous chapter, Chapter 10: Add Front-Matter Pages, might look something like this:

# Golden Nuggets

## Testimonial Pages

 Include                                    **Yes!**

 Aim for seven or eight testimonials

 Organize them:
- by impact to the reader
- by the testimonial writer's name and brand recognition
- to best benefit your business
- or a combination

## Title Page

 Always included                          **Yes!**

## Copyright Page

 Always included                          **Yes!**

## Dedication Page

 Optional

## Epigraph Page

 Optional, recommend excluding

## Table of Contents ("Contents")

  Nearly always included                    **Yes!**

## List of Illustrations, List of Tables

  Include only if needed

## Foreword

  Optional, recommended                    **Yes!**

## Preface

  Optional, recommend excluding

## Acknowledgments

  Optional, recommended                    **Yes!**

## Introduction

  Include if needed                        **Yes!**

# Chapter 12

---

# Add Back-Matter Pages

---

## End-of-Book Summary

As I mentioned in the previous chapter, if your book is fairly short—30K words or fewer—you might not have enough information in each chapter to need chapter summaries. Instead, you may opt to include an end-of-book summary, a two- or three-page compilation of the key points of the book, listed in order by chapter. You would place the summary in the back matter, the pages that follow your book's main text.

For example, *Business Gold*'s Part 1 summary might look like this:

---

# Key Points Summary

for

*Business Gold: How to Write a Book to Spotlight Your Expertise,*
*Attract a Ton of New Customers,*
*and Explode Your Profits!*

---

# Part 1
# Develop Your Concept

## Chapter 1
## The Two Keys to a Book's Success

A book's success depends on two key factors:

**1. Selling the book to potential readers**

**2. Inspiring those purchasers to network subsequent sales for you via enthusiastic word-of-mouth referrals**

How you develop, organize, write, and display the internal content determines the results your book will produce for the reader who purchased it, and whether he recommends it to his friends and colleagues.

## Chapter 2
## Develop Your Concept to Target Your Prospects

### 1. Your Brand

Branding is the art of making a unique and genuine promise and providing a unique experience for those your business serves.

### 2. Your Target Readers

They are the ones you most want to do business with—who most want to do business with you.

### 3. Your Book's Content

To make sure your book is successful bait, make sure it is bait (content) your prospects want. Need. Are hungry for.

## 4. Define Your Concept

Write your mission statement for your book.
Write your back-cover copy.
Always focus on how your readers will benefit.

## 5. Develop Your Concept

Make a list of the main topics and subtopics you will include in your book.
**Research Your Competitors**
**Revise Your Topics**
**Organize Your Topics**

## 6. Create Your Book Title

## 7. Create Chapter and Section Titles

Each chapter and section title should:
- succinctly and accurately convey the topic
- impact and excite the reader
- target your readers/prospects
- reflect your brand

## 8. Choose Your Book Style

Informational/How To
Business Biography
Allegory

Your end-of-book summary only needs to contain headers and the most important points. Remember, the goal for the summary is to emphasize key points so that they stick in the minds of your readers, and also to provide a handy reference so readers can easily locate information in the future. Keep it simple.

Business biographies and allegories typically do not include end-of-book summaries. Authors of those books may choose to underscore essential concepts, or provide action steps, at the end of each chapter, as we discussed in Chapter 11.

## Write the Chapter Summaries or End-of-Book Summary

Again, these summaries are optional. If you want to include either end-of-chapter summaries or an end-of-book summary, do so now. Or, you can have your manuscript editor do so for you. (Yes, that chapter on working with a manuscript editor is just ahead, in Chapter 14.)

## Appendix(es)

In an appendix, you can include side information related to the text that expands or clarifies a particular topic you discussed earlier in the book.

This section should not be used to discuss points that didn't fit elsewhere in the text. (*Appendix* means "appendage, something extra," not "the pesky stuff that didn't fit.")

For example, an appendix I might have added to this book could have been: MP3 Recorders I Recommend. (I didn't add this, because technology changes too quickly for that to be of benefit to you.)

Include an appendix only if its information will provide significant, added value to your reader.

## Glossary

If, in the book, you use foreign words or terms unfamiliar to your readers, use a glossary to provide helpful definitions.

Title the section Glossary, Key Terms, or similar wording.

Arrange words and terms alphabetically, each in **bold** type, followed by its definition in regular type. Here's an example of what entries typically look like when formatted:

---

**acid-free paper**. Paper having a pH of 7, or close to 7. Acid-free paper deteriorates at a much slower rate than paper with a lower pH, giving publications printed on it a longer life expectancy.

**adhesive binding**. A method of binding that employs glue instead of stitching to hold the pages or signatures together and is widely used for journals and paperback books. Three types of adhesive binding are currently used: perfect binding, notch binding, and burst binding.

---

(Source: *The Chicago Manual of Style*, 15<sup>th</sup> edition (Chicago: University of Chicago Press, 2003).)

Your manuscript editor can insert a glossary for you.

Business biographies and allegories typically do not include glossaries.

## Bibliography and/or References

If you would like to include a bibliography and/or a helpful list of references at the end of your book, simply send your manuscript editor the information, and they will format and add it to your manuscript's back matter for you. Or, you can easily insert it yourself.

Which information should you include? Books, articles, and other copyrighted references and their authors. You may choose to list those you haven't quoted directly from or mentioned previously, as well as those you quoted directly from.

For ideas—and access to phenomenal resources—see my References and Bibliography section in the back matter of *Business Gold*.

# Index

Indexes are usually unnecessary in books with word counts less than 50,000 when those books include detailed tables of contents, plentiful section headers, and chapter summaries or end-of-book summaries.

If your book is long (50,000 words or more), lacks end-of-chapter or end-of-book summaries, your readers might enjoy the handiness of an index.

Since my book walks you step-by-step through the book-production process so that you will have a published book in your hands after you turn the last page, I opted not to include an index.

An index can be difficult and time-consuming to produce with the accuracy needed to benefit your reader. An experienced professional indexer, possibly your manuscript editor, can provide this service for you.

Allegories typically do not include indexes.

# Bonus Section

Many authors of business books, particularly authors of informational/how-to books, like to gift their books' readers with bonus offers and discounts—juicy bait that will lure them right into the author's business funnel.

This bonus, or these bonuses, should be exciting enough to stimulate word-of-mouth advertising among your readers and their peers.

Create one or more special offers to deliver additional value (*always* over-deliver on value!), and to show readers product or service solutions you or your business provides—product or service solutions your book has revealed to them that they *need*.

Your goal with the bonus is *not* to generate immediate, regular-priced income, but to make readers' investments small enough and exciting enough to get them leaping onto your prospect hook.

They must see the bonus not as an obvious advertisement so that you can make more money from them, but as exceptional value you are giving to them that they cannot pass up.

One of the best uses of a bonus is to give readers a significant discount to your business's main product(s) or service(s).

If you wish, one of the bonuses can be a referral program that offers a reduction in your standard rate for each paid customer or client referred, up to a certain percentage less than your standard fee. Referral programs give the reader added incentive to enthusiastically tell others about your book and business.

You can also offer a discount on, or incentive for, quantity purchases of your book. Book promotion is essential to your book's success as bait to hook new clients. You can start promoting your book inside your book.

For the bonuses you offer, frame each one within an eye-catching border that reflects your brand, or simply provide a light-gray-shaded background. Keep written details short and simple, and use a font style and size that is easy to read.

To get a few ideas for wording and content—and to take advantage of valuable bonuses—see my Bonus! section at the end of the book.

Here are two examples of the visual element:

This is an example of a
framed
bonus offer.
Frames can be any size,
and have any
border style or shading.
Use a single frame,
or a box within a box
like this one.

This is another example of
a bonus offer.
It's set apart from regular text
by a gray-shaded background.

It can be as small as this one,
or it can fill the page.
When page-sized,
border lines are unnecessary,
since the page's white margins
neatly frame the gray.

Once readers sign on to participate in your free or deeply discounted session, coaching period, consultation, or other service or product, use that positive experience to net them as a new customer or client.

## About the Author

This biographical section nearly always appears at the very end of the book, unless the author is widely recognized and chooses to place the About the Author page in the front matter.

The About the Author page should be an expansion of your back-cover bio, and comparable to your Web site's About-you page.

Include, in any order that works well: your name, professional title, business name, years in business, related experience, tagline, prior publications, seminars and events for which you've been a speaker, special expertise if that hasn't been made clear in the book, notable awards, certifications, college degree(s) if relevant, and the like. Feel free to insert your black-and-white headshot.

You may also choose to mention the city and state of your business, and a word or two about your family. To connect with the reader in a personal way, include the name of your dog, cat, or iguana, and a fun, unexpected fact about the pet that the reader will identify with and remember. (I have thirteen parakeets. Few people forget a woman who has a parakeet habitat inside her home.)

Your About the Author page should be less than a page. Short and sweet. Don't get chatty and make the reader yawn now. This closing should be memorable and impressive.

You may choose to write it in first person (I, my) or third person (he, his). First person is more affable. Third person is more professional.

## And One More Thing . . .

After your back matter, you can choose to add one more page. Online reviews help to sell a book, yet few readers think to post a review. So, put the notion into their minds, by writing something like this:

If this book helped you, enhanced you, or even dazzled you,

kindly write a review at Amazon or B&N online,

tell others about this book,

and feel free to contact me with your own

testimonial for *Business Gold*

or personal success story with the book you authored, at

www.BusinessBookProductions.com.

Dedicated to your success,

*Tammy Barley*

The Millionaire Entrepreneurs' Book Consultant

## Write the Back Matter

Now, write any front and back matter that you haven't yet, and add it to your manuscript.

## Chapter 13

# How to Write
# Book-Cover Copy That Sells

The average potential buyer looks at the front cover of a book for no longer than eight seconds, and the back cover for no longer than fifteen, as I've mentioned. On your book covers, you'll need to provide great information fast.

## Front-Cover Copy

Only three groups of words appear on the front cover:

- Book title and subtitle, if any
- Author name
- One-line testimonial, usually shown in quotation marks, followed by the name of the person quoted; or, in its place, the name of the foreword contributor

Should you adopt a pen name? No. Since your professional goal for this book is to promote your business, the name you use in conjunction with your business should be placed on the cover. Make it easy for your prospects to locate and connect with you.

The one-line testimonial should concisely describe and praise the book. The name of the person who supplies the quote, or instead who contributes the foreword, should be a highly respected professional, a Big Name well known to the book's target audience.

The book title and Big Name should both compel the browser to read more.

## Book Spine

The spine displays the book title (usually without the subtitle, due to lack of space), author's name (last name only, if space is limited), and publisher's name, logo, or colophon (identifying emblem), again, depending on available space.

Unless the author's name is universally known, the book title should be the largest print on the spine.

Option: Ask your cover designer to use stacked letters for the book title, so that it is easily read among other titles on a bookstore or library shelf.

## Back-Cover Copy

Some of this will be a refresher from Chapter 2. Now that your manuscript writing is complete, go over the back-cover copy again to be sure it precisely sums up—and sells!—your content.

Remember, you'll have only seconds to hook your reader with your back-cover copy, so it must be brief, punchy, and list the main benefits or solutions your readers want.

### Headline

Begin with a short, one-sentence **headline** (a question or a statement) that captures your target reader. It should spotlight the potential reader's biggest problem or frustration, the primary solution that your potential reader needs and that your book provides.

If you grab your potential reader by the eyeballs with that first question or statement and evoke excitement, he will read more, or most of, the back cover. When done well, the headline alone goes a long way toward cinching the sale.

With that first line, you want your potential reader to think, *"This is the book I've been searching for!"*

Read the back-cover headlines of your favorite books. Analyze which headlines are the most compelling and why. Use that knowledge to inspire your headline.

Take all the time you need to create a strong, descriptive, compelling question or statement.

## Summary Paragraph

*"This* is the book I've been searching for!"

Continue to convince your potential reader of that with each subsequent line.

Beneath the headline, in a **summary paragraph** of four concise sentences or fewer, describe the main benefits or solutions your book provides. If you wrote your book for entrepreneurs and other business professionals who consistently invest time to read and learn, you can add a couple of more sentences.

Remember: Great information fast. If you *can* summarize the book in one short paragraph, or even one sentence, do it.

Show the potential reader that the book provides valuable information worth exponentially more than the amount they will invest in the book. Pinpoint the benefits of time, money, or other benefits the reader will either save or gain as a result of this purchase.

## Bulleted List

Beneath the summary paragraph, use a **bulleted list** to briefly detail the other top benefits or solutions readers will gain.

## Summary Line

Add a final **summary line** that delivers a compelling burst of excitement or notable value for the potential reader.

## To Sum Up

Use short paragraphs, short sentences, bulleted points, and accentuate benefits and value, to ensure that the potential reader cannot put your book down.

Try to complete all of the above back-cover copy in 150 words or fewer.

Since this is one of your primary selling points, invest the time to make it perfect. Have associates read it and give their reaction. When you peg the needle on the enthusiasm meter, the summary is done.

## Back-Cover Testimonials

Beneath your copy, insert two to four brief, powerful **testimonials** by Big Names in your field, well known to your readers. (Five or more start to become too many to read.) Those Big Names will also help sell your book.

Below each name, include their business name, title, professional tagline if you have space, and business URL. You could also add a top-selling book they've published or another notable achievement.

## Your Mini Biography

Also on the back cover, your **mini bio** will appear, placed either:

- beneath the testimonials a few inches from the bottom, leaving enough space for the bar code
- or to the right of the book-summary paragraph and bulleted list

Your cover artist will have ideas for placement.

Head the mini bio with your name, and professional tagline if you have space.

Your bio should be very short—one paragraph, just a few sentences—since the reader will merely skim it. In addition to your name, insert only the details that will reveal your expertise—why you are the *one* to write this book, why you are the *one* the reader needs to learn from.

If space allows, add your professional title and the name of your business. For example: [Your Name] is founder/owner/CEO, etc. of ___ (insert your business name), provider of ___ solutions for ___ (target customer).

Follow that with your business's URL, if space allows.

Beneath that, add your book's URL—again, if space allows.

In your mini bio, include only the most compelling information in order to reveal yourself as an expert. That expert status will encourage the sale of the book. Your About the Author page in the back matter can be more detailed.

Include a professionally photographed, full-color headshot, an inch and a half across or tall at most, a photo that suggests your brand and connects with your core audience, so that readers can link a trusted face with your name. (Omit the headshot if a photo of you appears on the front cover.)

So, to sum up, your back-cover bio should include:

- your name
- your full-color headshot
- details that reveal your expertise/why you're the one the reader needs to learn from

### On the Bottom

Beneath your bio, your cover artist will need to insert:

- ISBN
- bar code
- retail price
- optional: name of the book's publishing company (even if it's your own made-up publishing company—discussed in Chapter 23) and its URL

You may also opt to have your cover artist add a small banner advertising one of your bonus materials. The banner can appear across the top of the back cover, near the bottom, or diagonally across the upper, outer corner of the book cover.

Try to complete all of the back-cover copy in 250 words or fewer.

## Dust Jacket

If you plan to publish your book in a hardcover edition (see related section in Chapter 21), your book may need a dust jacket.

A dust jacket contains the same basic copy as a soft-cover book, but parts of it are arranged differently.

Choose from the following two style options. Use whichever works best for you.

### Option One

The dust jacket's front looks the same as the front cover of a soft-cover book.

The spine looks the same.

The back looks partly the same—headline, summary paragraph, bulleted list, summary line, and two to four testimonials by Big Names and/or reviewers. Also, ISBN, bar code, price, URLs.

On the front flap, a more detailed summary of the book is placed.

On the back flap is where your mini bio goes. Usually, the credit for dust jacket design is placed beneath your bio, and often publisher information as well.

### Option Two

The dust jacket's front looks the same as the front cover of a soft-cover book.

The spine looks the same.

The back looks partly the same—headline, one- or two-line summary of the book's main solution or tagline, followed by testimonials and/or reviews. Also, ISBN, bar code, price, URLs.

On the front flap, a more detailed summary of the book is placed, beginning with a new headline. (Do not duplicate the headline from the back cover. Keep it fresh. Keep the potential reader glued.)

On the back flap is where your mini bio goes. Usually, the credit for dust jacket design is placed beneath your bio, and often publisher information as well.

## Complete Your Back-Cover Copy or Dust-Jacket Copy

Complete your back-cover copy, or dust-jacket copy, now. When it is publication-ready, then read on.

Go ahead. I'll wait.

If your book isn't business gold yet, it's about to be. In the next chapter, I'll discuss working with a manuscript editor, that book expert who can make your manuscript golden . . . and free up your time and make the rest of your book-production process easier.

# Chapter 14

# Editor: The Golden Key to Your Book's Success

You're now ready to send your masterpiece to a manuscript editor. If you haven't included all of the front or back matter yet, no worries. Your manuscript editor can insert it, and polish it, for you.

The manuscript editor. This is one expert you absolutely need. Every writer must have this second set of eyes, this writing and book-production guru. A professional editor, and not merely a proofreader who puts commas in the right places. Here's why.

## Organization

Most completed manuscripts, even if well organized at the outset, become disorganized in the rewriting process. After a manuscript has been written and read, rewritten and read again, and the writer has tweaked a number of versions, his external words and internal brainstorming have amalgamated into a brain soup of what he wants to say. The author rewrites, thinks of a point to add, and doesn't recall that he made a similar point several chapters earlier. Even with careful self-editing, identical topics get discussed more than once, which confuses the reader as well as the point the author intended to make.

After rereading and rewriting, it's no longer possible for the author to view the finished manuscript from a new reader's perspective.

It happens to virtually ever author, to one extent or another, in virtually every book. This even happens to me when I write a book. It's the nature of the writing beast.

Each author needs the sharp eyes of an editor highly experienced with content organization to streamline and simplify the finished content, so that it provides the best possible value to the reader.

## Concept Development

Speakers who write books must develop their written topics differently than they would if speaking those topics to an audience. Think about it. As a speaker, you can touch on various points at different times, and the audience will still follow your line of conversation. "We'll talk more about X, Y, and Z in a few minutes. But first . . ." This can be beneficial while speaking, and your audience hears, momentarily anticipates, and then easily disengages from X, Y, and Z, and next absorbs what you say about A, B, and C. If you mention a point before or after you intended to, your audience simply takes it in. They understand it.

The same is true for all business professionals who talk with customers or clients, but who might not be proficient book writers for audiences of readers.

Book readers never disengage. They mentally file every point, in the order each point is presented.

You've likely heard the fiction-writers' axiom, "If you introduce a revolver in chapter one, a character had better fire it by chapter two." The reason for this is that the reader mentally snatches up each new detail, a detail such as a senator slipping a gun into the inner pocket of his coat, and then the reader waits in anticipation for the author to reveal the subsequent fact about that element.

The reader's primary focus is now on that revolver. He expects it to fire. He needs it to fire. He can't pay attention to another four or five chapters of unrelated events while waiting for that gun's purpose to be revealed.

Careful concept development in a nonfiction book is just as critical to a reader. Similar to organization, concept development involves how each topic in a book is expanded, step by step, and how close together the steps of that expansion are presented. Four or five chapters is too long to wait to learn the destiny of that revolver. Or to wait for a book's author to add more information about a topic you care about that has only been mentioned in passing.

However, if there is no way around this—say, if various topics are interconnected—then simply develop each topic as clearly and logically as possible. This was the approach I took in *Business Gold*.

Also, the senator can't fire the gun if the reader never sees him put it in his pocket. Likewise, your readers won't easily understand the expansion of a point if the initial point has not yet been made. It happens often in business book manuscripts (and in fiction manuscripts too).

Most concept-development problems are avoided when a book is outlined in advance. But if a book was added to during rewrites, as often happens, concept development will almost certainly be affected.

A manuscript editor will ensure your content is well organized and well developed. (And they'll make sure the senator slides the revolver out of his pocket by chapter two.)

## Business-Book Writing Expertise

So, an experienced editor excels at presenting information in a logical and flowing format.

He or she is also a ghostwriter, and uses advanced writing skills (particularly if they have a background as a fiction author) to make your content sing. He or she grips the reader with a fresh voice, vivid sensory narrative, and employs dozens of other fiction and nonfiction writing techniques to ensure the content has maximum sticking power.

Additionally, the editor ghostwrites for maximum smoothness, transitions, simplifying, and tightening, to ensure the manuscript is fresh, timely, and continually engages the reader.

He or she can advise you on, or help you write, front- and back-matter sections and the back-cover copy, and assist you with virtually every other manuscript detail.

Most importantly, a good nonfiction editor will have years of experience assisting entrepreneurs and business professionals like yourself to write and edit successful books, so that satisfied readers will see you as *the* leading expert. The one they must gain further assistance from.

Simply put, an expert business-book editor is the golden key to producing a book that nets rave reviews and recommendations . . . and turns readers into presold prospects that stream into your business funnel.

## How to Find an Editor Who Has Business-Book Writing Expertise

Fortunately, an author's rewrites and self-editing does bring about a good manuscript. By following the techniques in *Business Gold*, his manuscript is now a shimmering 18-karat work. It stands apart from literally thousands of dull 10-karat documents.

An editor skilled in advanced business-book techniques will refine that 18-karat script to 24 karat—pure. Dazzling. In demand.

One of the most well-known online resources for finding a large pool of editors to select from is www.Elance.com. At such online resource pools, you post information about your project, and interested editors bid. Perhaps you can already see the challenges here. Although several in each pool of editors are top-notch, anyone can hang out a shingle and call himself an editor, and anyone hungry for a job will bid.

Bids will range from $5 per hour to $500 per hour, and many projects receive a hundred bids or more. Is the $5-per-hour bidder worth only that little? Is the $500-per-hour bidder worth that much? Which of them is truly knowledgeable?

To find out, research each bidder—their page at the resource site, their portfolio of published books that they've assisted with, their one-to five-star ratings given by past clients, client recommendations, and visit their Web site(s) on the World Wide Web to learn even more about them. It takes time to research each bidder, and there will be dozens of them.

Once you have thinned the options to a final handful, you communicate with each via a private message board then select one editor from there.

Fishing in an online resource pool takes time, but that is the most common option.

In addition to Elance.com, other well-known online resource pools include oDesk.com, iFreelance.com, Guru.com, and TaskArmy.com.

You can also ask colleagues who have written books if they can recommend an editor.

## Thousand-Dollar Tip

Save weeks of time and relieve all stress and uncertainty. See how Business Book Production's team can assist you to turn your manuscript concept into an expertly written, edited, graphics-enhanced self-published book you can place into your prospects' hands. For more information about our programs that partner you with guidance and experience at every step, visit www.BusinessBookProductions.com.

Your goal as an entrepreneur is to devote your valuable time doing what you do best. So, bring a business-book editorial expert on board for your manuscript project, and allow him or her to do what they do best.

And that leads me to this chapter's final topic.

## All Those Pesky Details

As I mentioned early in this chapter, sending your manuscript to any available proofreader or editor won't get your book the expertise it must have.

An experienced editor can also proofread, of course, but a sentence's impact (or lack of it) depends on that editor knowing the difference between the "correct" place to insert a comma and the *best* place to insert it. What's best for the sentence (and paragraph, chapter, and book) is often not what your fifth-grade English teacher said is "correct." Actually, a number of those old "rules" are considered antiquated and are no longer done.

The comma was just one example. The same is true for every minute detail of your book.

While proofreading, an editor focuses on thousands of proofreading and formatting details—twelve formatting and continuity checks just for one, individual chapter header! They truly work to make your book the most professional it can be, so that your reader becomes a presold prospect who trusts that your business will be just as exceptional.

In addition to everything else you've learned that an editor does, here are other details he sees to:

**Copyedit**

If the meaning of a sentence is unclear, or if a section will benefit from different paragraph breaks, editors make the update. Word or phrase repetitions (such as all those uses of –ing)? Corrected. As ghostwriters, they rephrase where needed to smoothen, simplify, tighten, and assure natural transitions.

**Proofread**

A final proofread will catch errors in spelling, capitalization, punctuation, basic grammar (subject-verb agreement), spacing, and other mistakes at the sentence level. It will also provide consistency in spelling (traveled or travelled), capitalizations (Miss or miss), hyphens or dashes (- or –), abbreviations (Dr., Doctor, or doctor), numbers (125 or one hundred twenty-five), as well as verify consistency of format— both written layout and graphics formatting—throughout.

## Editor: The Difference between Failure and Success

You might have heard of both AP style and Chicago style. Do you know when each is used? (Answer: AP style is used for articles; Chicago is used for books.) I come across editors who are unaware of this.

A good book editor is fluent in Chicago style. For correctness and continuity of spelling, they refer to *Merriam-Webster's Collegiate Dictionary*, the most recent edition. Those two resources are *the* publishing industry standards. Having an editor fluent in the application of these resources is like having a translator fluent in the language of a country where you must do business.

As I've said, an experienced business-manuscript editor is the one book professional no author can do without. This is critical to understand. Asking your spouse, a friend, or even an English teacher to edit for you will not produce the creative or professional results you and your business need.

Choose your editor wisely. Your editor will not merely affect your book. Your editor will affect the results it has on your business.

Another reason to choose your editor wisely? More and more entrepreneurs have begun to discover that authoring a book enables them to spotlight themselves as leaders in their fields. True industry leaders, those whom customers mentally place on a pedestal, will be those who produce more than one book. Having an editor you know and trust, and who knows you and understands your business, will enable you to quickly produce a second book, and any others after that.

Producing a new book every year or two will help you maintain a lead position in your industry.

Subsequent books also add branches to your pipeline, and they create loyal customers or clients who keep buying from you since you keep providing the solutions they need.

Loyal customers means reliable, long-term profits and ongoing referrals from those who enjoy doing business with you.

Getting customers means you make a sale. Keeping them means they have exponentially more lifetime value.

So, while you're finishing your first book, consider what to include in your second and third books, and keep a list of those ideas. When your next manuscript is complete, you'll already have a trusted editor who can help you to make it a success.

Connect with an editor now. To assist you, I've included an "Editor Qualifications Sheet" on the following page. Have the manuscript editor you choose edit your manuscript and get it publication-ready.

While they're doing that, you can advance to the next step— graphic artistry.

# Editor Qualifications Sheet

✓ **All business-book editors you consider should have the following qualifications:**

| | |
|---|---|
| | Experience editing your style of business book: informational/how to, business biography, or allegory |
| | Published fiction author, particularly if your book is an allegory |
| | Experience editing for your audience |

✓ **You need your editor to assist with (check all that apply):**

| | |
|---|---|
| | ghostwriting—turning your notes into a manuscript for you |
| | content edit (content organization and concept development) |
| | copyedit |
| | proofread |
| | fluent in Chicago style |
| | help with brainstorming book, chapter, and section titles, titles for your callout boxes |
| | end-of-chapter summaries |
| | end-of-book summary |
| | glossary |
| | bibliography and/or list of references |
| | index (a specialty; few editors are also indexers) |
| | interior layout:<br>• format all elements of text (appearance on page)<br>• add and format graphics (appearance on page) |
| | back-cover copy |
| | proofread/edit book-cover text |
| | add LCCN information to copyright page |
| | publishing format(s)—i.e., traditional, self-, and/or e-publishing—that you will use for your book |
| | query letter, synopsis, proposal |
| | press release |
| | blog posts |
| | magazine articles |
| | media package for reviewers and the media |
| | a project coordinator to quarterback manuscript production for you |

Part 4

# Creative Artistry
# to Attract a Ton of New Customers

# Chapter 15

## Interior Graphics: Styles and Applications

We've seen that a book's success depends on two key factors:
1. Selling the book to potential readers
2. Inspiring those purchasers to network subsequent sales for you via enthusiastic word-of-mouth referrals

A book's title and cover art alone inspire a potential reader's initial wow-factor with the book. That wow-factor compels the potential reader to skim the back cover and, if the cover copy grips him, several pages inside. There, interior graphics, if done well, will expand the potential reader's interest.

Exterior and interior wow-factor can help to sell the book.

It can also begin to create a bond between the reader and the book, which you as the author augment with great writing on every page.

The book cover is the first—and one of the most critical—feature that hooks a potential reader and prospect.

And through him, his network of friends and connections.

Now that your manuscript editor has begun his or her work, it's time to connect with a book-cover artist and graphic designer.

Often, one artist can provide the visual elements for both the exterior and interior of your book. You can work with one artist for both, or two independent artists, whichever is best for you.

One artist will ensure the art style and techniques are identical inside and outside your book, if that is of paramount importance to your audience and goals.

Two independent artists can often bring about results that are similar to each other in style, and can finish the visual elements quicker, if speed is important.

Working with two artists will require more extensive communication, since you may need to arrange three-party communications once or twice. So, the communication may take longer, but the art itself can go faster with two artists doing the work.

Again, it is your choice entirely.

We'll talk about cover art in detail in the next chapter. For now, we'll focus on interior graphics, so that you can examine creative artistry on a smaller scale, before moving on to advanced concepts.

In this chapter I'll add several extra graphic elements, in order to demonstrate fresh ways to use them, and to inspire your own creativity to develop engaging elements that you can use in your book.

## After the Reader's Purchase: Why Interior Graphics Are Essential to Your Book's Success

With the ongoing influence of the Internet, smartphones, and other communication and information mediums that rely heavily on visuals to convey topics and their meanings, graphics in both print and e-books are now more important than ever. In fact, illustrations, even cartoon-style images, are steadily gaining in popularity, even in business books.

Business-book readers read to learn. These folks are, in part, visual learners. In addition to immersing themselves in written text, visual learners also like to watch live demonstrations and videos, and to see simple illustrations that make new concepts easy to understand and remember.

Illustrations of key points add visual appeal to a book. They grab the reader's attention and also bolster his interest in the content. They enable your reader to further enjoy the experience your book provides.

Books that do not include interior graphics can seem less interesting, less engaging to the reader. More like a textbook. Two dimensional.

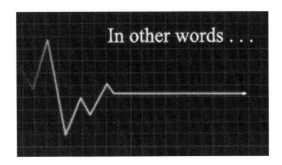

Illustrations generate three-dimensional intrigue, and deliver long-term learning. You might not recall exactly the words an author used to explain a concept, but you likely remember the graphic representation of that concept.

Memorable concepts, due to memorable graphics, leave lasting impressions. Lasting value. Books with lasting value get recommended, and then the authors, and their businesses, get noticed in a big way.

Premium interior graphics contribute to your book's success.

Your book: Fat, juicy bait.

Here are four main kinds of interior graphics and their uses. Select one or more for your book, based on your goals, audience, and communication needs. Consult with your graphic artist to be sure the creative elements you want to use will work well together.

## Custom Graphic Representations

The Food Guide Pyramid. We still remember the original graphic representation of this concept that we studied in grade school—foods our bodies need less of (fats, oils, sweets) at the small, triangular top of the pyramid, and foods our bodies need in greater quantities (bread, cereal, rice, pasta) along the large pyramid base.

In recent years, a new Food Guide Pyramid graphic was introduced, which many people are still scratching their heads about. The new graphic isn't as easy to understand, or remember, as the original.

The original, however, instantly comes to mind, even after all these years since grade school. That is an effective graphic.

As an entrepreneur, you might already use several custom graphic representations to instruct your customers, clients, or members of your team. If you've already had an artist produce quality graphics for your brochures or sales materials, perhaps use those in your book. If not, any basic geometric shape(s) you've drawn on a paper napkin to illustrate a concept can be converted into a custom graphic representation for your book (and for use in your brochures and sales materials).

In addition to pyramids or triangles, these graphics can also be wheels with spokes, a circle of actions or events, a target, a compass, rectangles to represent steps to a new level, a vertical cylinder like a trash can (without top or bottom) to represent the professional equivalent of "garbage in, garbage out," and the like.

Or, instead of geometric shapes, use simple machines—a wedge, lever, inclined plane, pulley, or screw—such as gears to depict interdependent components.

Of course, you are not limited to basic geometric shapes and simple machines. In their book *Midas Touch*, authors Donald Trump and Robert T. Kiyosaki use the palm of a hand with its five digits, one thumb and four fingers, to illustrate the five points of their Midas touch—what you need to know to succeed as an entrepreneur. (The book's title is a play on words that correlates both to the legend of Midas and to the sense of touch depicted by the hand graphic. This connection would have been lost if the image had been of the back of the hand and fingernails, which do not feel the sense of touch like the pads of the fingers do. It would have been a somewhat less effective graphic than it is.)

Use in whole, or the parts of, a body—human, animal, mechanical (such as a tractor)—or aspects of another object your readers have common knowledge of. All can be effective graphics if done well.

Do you *need* to include custom graphic representations in your book? Not at all. You can use other visual elements, such as those I will describe on the following pages, to create reader interest and to make your information stick.

However, if one or more graphic representations is the best way to achieve reader interest and information impact, then definitely use it. The more interesting the graphic, the more its concept will resonate, and the more memorable it will be.

Graphic representations often include short phrases and/or icons.

Brainstorm with your artist to produce images that will clearly and memorably illustrate each concept you want to represent. As always, keep in mind the business brand you want to convey.

An additional brand element that Trump and Kiyosaki's hand graphic represents is hard work. An open hand also represents honesty and forthrightness.

Any icons or drawn objects/people must be very basic in construction, even when reduced in size, so that they print clearly when your book is published. Use your word processor's page size function to see the actual size that the art will be when published.

Since you will likely print your book in black and white, your illustrations will be grayscale shading rather than color, though you can ask your artist to also provide the graphics in color so that you can use them in your e-book, business materials, and Web site.

Sample of a two-dimensional graphic.    Sample of a three-dimensional graphic.

Ask your artist to design the style of graphic that works best for you.

How many different custom graphic representations can you include? At most, I recommend no more than three or four per book, or they may become too numerous to be memorable. Another option is that you can use one basic design, then vary it in a number of places in your book.

For example, if you use four adjoining rectangles to represent the four steps needed to reach an outcome, each step can be shaded in the chapter that discusses it. Shade the next step in the next chapter, and so on.

Graphic representations work best in informational/how-to books and business biographies.

As with all graphics, invest the time and resources to do them right. Produce the best graphic to illustrate your concept and to make it memorable.

## Callout Boxes

Also known as text boxes, these are visibly framed bits of text that appear between paragraphs or to the left or right of regular page text. The callout boxes were so named because they call out for a reader's attention.

This is a simple callout box.

This is a simple callout box with light-gray shading.

My Thousand-Dollar Tips appear in callout boxes:

### Thousand-Dollar Tip

This is a more eye-catching callout box. It includes a decorative border, light gray shading, and a graphic element—stacks of gold coins.

Callout boxes add visual interest, and they also spotlight ancillary information.

Some authors use them solely to repeat blocks of page text word for word throughout their books. I don't recommend this.

Why not? Because the purpose of the callout box is to add interest—visual and *mental* interest. Repetition is not mentally interesting, in the same way that a dripping faucet is not audibly interesting. An author can use a couple of his callout boxes to emphasize a few key points, but most callout boxes should be used to provide something new.

Text inside callout boxes may be helpful tips, inspiring quotes, a side fact related to the text, an intriguing or impactful statistic, URLs that provide more information or assistance (especially your URLs), and so on.

Callout boxes deliver added value. In fact, think of them as *added-value boxes*. They also give the reader brief mental breathers from the blocks of great information you infuse him with on every page.

Callout boxes work best in informational/how-to books and business biographies. It's best to insert them between paragraphs or to one side, so that they don't interrupt the reader's concentration in the middle of a concept or sentence.

As I mentioned, visually-appealing callout boxes often include graphics. Robert Skrob, in his book *The Official Get Rich Guide to Information Marketing: Build a Million-Dollar Business within 12 Months*, Second Edition, simply uses a lock-and-keys graphic inside an upper corner of his callout boxes. The callout boxes are aptly titled "Key Concept."

Also, callout boxes might not be boxes at all. They might be graphics themselves. In *Who Moved My Cheese?*, the callout box is a wedge of Swiss cheese that serves as a backdrop to a line or two of written text.

In Dan Kennedy's book *No B.S. Business Success in the New Economy*, the callout box is two adjoining stone tablets shaped like those bearing the Ten Commandments God gave to Moses. Dan Kennedy's ten-commandment-style callout boxes are titled "Dan Kennedy's Eternal Truth #___." The font looks like letters etched in stone. His callout boxes inject a dose of humor, are unique and therefore striking, and also present an element of solid wisdom that adds value for the reader. The callout box helps to make Dan Kennedy's book enjoyable to read, and memorable. And because the shading of the stone is faint and contrasts the dark letter font, all wording is easy to read.

> A callout box can be any shape, and can be positioned anywhere on the page.

Artistic style and valuable content. That is the result of an effective callout box.

Page through your favorite books. What callout-box graphics and titles did the authors use? With those ideas to inspire you, work with a graphic artist to come up with fresh ideas for yours.

Fresh ideas can include:

- **variations to simple, rectangular callout boxes** (such as rounded or angled corners)
- **variations to the frame's lines** (narrower or thicker lines, or even a box within a box, such as those used in the Bonus! section)
- **"boxes" that are graphics themselves** (like the soccer ball)
- **various patterns and amounts of shading** (if any)

Do callout boxes *have* to include graphics? Not at all. You can easily enclose special tips or side information in a straightforward, rectangular callout box, and the box can be shaded or not, like the two examples of "simple callout boxes" that you saw at the beginning of this section. Do whatever works best for your book goals and audience.

Callout-box titles, if you want to title them, often hint at your business's brand. Talk with your editor to brainstorm titles for your callout boxes.

Should you left- or full-justify your callout box text? Should the text be centered? Answer: Work with your artist to determine what looks best.

Should you use a font other than the book's text font? Should you use a smaller font than the book's text font uses? Typically, the callout-box font is smaller than the book's text font, and is a sans serif font so that this smaller text is clear and easy to read. Again, work with your artist to determine what works best.

In the event you're wondering, serifs are the tiny curls or lines at the edges of letters. Sans serif fonts do not have the curls, such as Ariel or Calibri. Calibri 10-point is the font I use in my Thousand-Dollar Tip callout boxes.

Serif fonts (with curls) are used for a book's main text, because the curls lead the reader's eyes easily across the page. Sans Serif fonts (without curls) are used for headers, because they momentarily stop the eye.

Should you indent paragraphs or add a space between them? Single space the lines or use 1.15 line spacing? You already know what I'm going to say—work with you artist to determine what looks and works best.

I indent my text-box paragraphs five character spaces. Lines are 1.15 spacing.

# Thousand-Dollar Tip

Consider having your artist design different callout boxes for each book you write, even if only the borders differ, so that each book has fresh visual appeal. Remember, repetition will bore the reader, but you'll captivate them each time you deliver something new.

## Diagrams

In many informational/how-to books, diagrams are necessary. If your book teaches mechanically-challenged people how to perform basic car maintenance, you'll need to include simple diagrams of a car's body and engine. Diagrams are often labeled with parts or steps.

Should you use a cartoon-like diagram, or a more realistic diagram? That depends on your audience, though a morsel of creativity will provide a more unique and enjoyable experience for the reader. However, if you're going for a direct, information-only approach, stick with a realistic style.

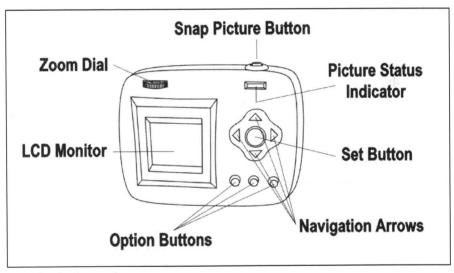

Example of a diagram for a camera.

## Cartoons

A cartoon is an often lighthearted depiction of a setting, person or character, object, or snapshot of a scene.

Cartoons (one-frame style rather than strips) add visual interest and content value to allegorical books. Allegorical stories present symbology, metaphor, and added meaning beyond the obvious. The illustrations can be used to depict a person, place, or object as well as their layers of symbolism. So, quality cartoon images in allegorical books can be a powerful way to impart wisdoms as well as their significance.

In informational/how-to books and business biographies, cartoons can be used to entertain a reader and provide him with a brief mental break from the text. A scenic highway is a beautiful thing, but rest stops are wonderful places to unbuckle and stretch the legs.

"No, we're not claiming this planet, boys. We're just stretching our legs."

As with other interior graphics, use diagrams or cartoons in any way you need them—to educate, entertain, disarm, inspire. Diagrams and cartoons are creative and versatile tools, though note that they are both rarely used together in the same book.

How many diagrams should you include? As many as you need. Add clear, concise captions if they will help to explain the illustration.

How many cartoons? No more than one per chapter. If each cartoon is placed on a page of its own, include a caption to anchor the illustration, so that it does not visually float around the page space.

Like custom graphic representations, any drawn objects or characters must be fairly basic in construction, especially when reduced in size, so that they print clearly when your book is published. Use your word processor's page-size function to see the actual size each illustration will be when published.

Since you will likely print your book in black and white, your illustrations will be grayscale shading rather than color. Your graphic designer should send you grayscale drawings so that you know exactly how each will appear when your book is printed.

Be sure the drawings or cartoons mesh with your book goals, audience, and brand.

If you need ideas for what diagrams or cartoons to include, a good graphic artist will have ideas in abundance.

## Charts and Graphs

Charts and graphs tend to be more logical in nature than creative. Thus, they tend to be more informative than interesting. Since you want to keep your readers captivated, try to use charts or graphs only when absolutely necessary, and work with your graphic artist to conceptualize ways to add clean visual interest to them so that they draw attention. Be sure the charts or graphs are simple to understand, and that any text will be easy to read when published.

For example, here is a visually and intellectually interesting pie chart that a chiropractor might use in his book, so that prospective patients who have these injuries will see him as the ideal chiropractic care provider:

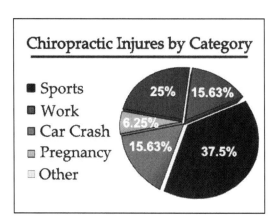

Since you will likely print your book in black and white, your charts or graphs will be grayscale shading rather than color. Your graphic designer should send you grayscale drawings so that you know exactly how each will appear in print.

How many charts or graphs should you include? No more than two or three per book. If you can communicate the necessary information within the book's text in a way that is effortless for the reader to understand, then do so. If charts or graphs are the best means, then use these visual tools.

## Visual Brand

Visual brand in interior graphics is a matter of image choice and the unique style of representing that image.

Logos are simple visuals, but we'll use two to show the power of creative artistry.

Consider the Nike swoosh. That illustration conveys speed and movement. It is swift. It is basic. It is a brilliant representation of

Nike's brand of performance, both for themselves as producers and for their customers.

Or let your mind draw the three circles of Mickey Mouse's head and ears that represent the Walt Disney Company. A symbol of completeness and entertainment, of people who create with *their* heads and listen with *their* ears, so that everyone else can enjoy with theirs. One glance at those three circles, and your lightened heart is standing at the wide-open gates of the Magic Kingdom.

Those are simple logos, yet they are powerful visual brands.

The *Who Moved My Cheese?* wedge of Swiss cheese has come to represent the authors' brand of providing superior food for thought. The V-shaped wedge replaces the V in the book's title, and in the titles of other books in that series. Now, information-seekers know to head straight to the big cheese.

You can likewise contribute an aura of your brand to the illustrations you choose, through their subject matter and the way that subject is artistically designed.

When you select a graphic designer, be sure they can work with you to provide any visual branding assistance you need. Not every graphic must represent your brand overtly, but each should create a subtle image in readers' minds of the kind of person you are and the kind of business you have developed.

If you and your business are down-to-earth in tone and enjoyable to work with, cartoons can be an effective medium to visually communicate that. If you and your business are dedicated to your clients' wealth and success, choose appropriate visuals to inspire that knowledge.

## Your Book's Graphics

In Chapter 2, you researched several aspects of your competitors' published books and bookmarked their Web pages, for future reference. If you need additional ideas to help you brainstorm interior graphics for your book, return to those books' Web pages now, look inside the books, and use their visual elements to inspire your ideas.

Interior graphics add creative interest and often informational value to your book. They are a great way to connect with your reader, and to inspire word-of-mouth, must-read referrals.

If you need more ideas still, your graphic artist will have them.

# Chapter 16

# Book-Cover Artistry: Interview with Graphic Designer Jim Saurbaugh

Right now, your manuscript editor is polishing the chapters and words of your opus to a golden finish. You can almost envision it, touch it—your published book. It's much more than paper and ink. It's your knowledge, your effort, the next exciting addition to the business you've worked this long to build.

Your opus is one spectacular book cover away from being published. From there, it's only a delivery truck away from being held in your hands.

So let's get you a spectacular book cover.

You can design a book cover in one of three ways.

1. Do-it-yourself template
2. Your publisher or self-publishing company can design it for you
3. Select and work with a professional cover designer

# Cover-Design Option #1: Do-It-Yourself Template

Big meeting, about to begin. Prospective clients to impress. You've worked years for this opportunity.

You're about to open the door, step into the conference room, and sell them on all that your business has to offer.

You're wearing your power suit. Silk tie. Italian leather shoes. You emanate Humphrey Bogart charisma.

You pull the door handle, smile your megawatt grin, and stride into the room.

Greetings all around, then you place a copy of your new book—your newest personal achievement—onto the gleaming cherrywood surface of the conference table, the book you've told them so much about.

With interest, their eyes lower to the book—this paragon of your years of expertise—and stare . . . at the milk-curdling do-it-yourself cover art.

The cover art that some devil-may-care blogger assured his readers they could do themselves in a single weekend with a simple template program.

The only sound in the room is that of your longed-awaited opportunity colliding with the floor.

Expressions go carefully blank all around, but you can read the pervading thought: *Should've spent as much on the cover as you did on your tie, pal.*

Fortunately, this is only a dream.

This *is* a dream, right? Any moment now your alarm clock will ring, and it will all be over.

Any moment now. The clock will ring.

*Ring, blast it!*

Suddenly, a single, horrible thought knifes through the emotional nuclear detonation:

You. Are. Awake.

The moral of the story?

Unless you are a gifted artist experienced with visual branding and dozens of other nuances of book-cover artistry, avoid—like you would avoid a pit of crocodiles—do-it-yourself book-cover templates.

## Cover-Design Option #2: Publisher Designed

If you publish through a traditional brick-and-mortar publisher, they design your cover for you. You get to provide little, if any, input. Good luck with that.

If you self-publish, many self-publishing companies offer cover-design services. In fact, that's frequently included in the price of your publishing package. Five or so hours of design time (perhaps with a template program), a choice of two covers, one image chosen by the designer. Or sometimes, you can provide a selection of images, and they can choose from those or from other images in their image library.

Still doesn't give you a lot of options. Or a lot of confidence.

Unless your self-publishing company consistently produces outstanding book-cover artistry, I recommend hiring your own experienced and vetted artist.

## Cover-Design Option #3: Professional Cover Artist

. . . You place a copy of your new book—your newest personal achievement—onto the gleaming cherrywood surface of the conference table, the book you've told them so much about.

With interest, their eyes lower to the book—this paragon of your years of expertise—and stare . . . then, simultaneously, they reach for the impressive-looking copy.

You wrote the contents, had it edited, and had the cover professionally designed, to attract a ton of new customers. The exterior wow-factor is doing just that.

That is an effective cover design.

## Top 2 Cover-Design Secrets

Your artist will be a great idea-stormer, but here are two top-selling secrets to keep in mind.

1. The book title font should be easy to read at a glance, both on the front cover and on the spine, so don't get carried away with the font style. Font can be as off-putting as bad cover art, or it can add commanding wow-factor.

2. If you anticipate your book reaching a wide audience (selling hundreds of thousands of copies) or winning a notable award or other recognition (recognition should be one of your goals), have your cover designer leave space on the front for a gold medallion, like the medallions on award certificates. In subsequent editions, your designer can add a medallion with wording that announces the recognition. Use this tip carefully; falsified or insignificant recognition will work against you, and against your business. When used to demonstrate actual merit, such medallions frequently rocket book sales to an all-new level.

# Interview with Graphic Designer Jim Saurbaugh

As an editor, I've been privileged to work on several previous books for which Jim has provided brilliant, eye-grabbing cover art.

A number of graphic artists can produce superior cover designs. I selected Jim Saurbaugh to interview for one significant reason: He has the ability to precisely capture the author's brand, content, writing style, and target audience, all with one design.

Graduate of The Pennsylvania School of Art & Design and a commercial art specialist, Jim is owner of J.S. Graphic Design in Lancaster County, Pennsylvania.

He typically doesn't do interior graphics for books—covers are his passion—but since he has years of design expertise, I asked him questions about interior graphics as well, which he was happy to answer.

**Tammy Barley:** Jim, thank you for taking the time to share your creative know-how. My readers and I appreciate it.

**Jim Saurbaugh:** Absolutely. How often can you talk about yourself without looking conceited?

**Tammy Barley:** (Laughs.) What first inspired you to work with authors and provide cover designs for their books?

**Jim Saurbaugh:** I was referred to an author by another client, and he asked if I had ever done a book cover before. I had to say, "No, but I'd love to do it anyway." Now I have several under my belt.

**Tammy Barley:** At what point during the book-production process should an author contact you for assistance with the cover design?

**Jim Saurbaugh:** I would say as soon as you have your title finalized, let me know. Then, while you are working on the content of the book, I have time to research your book subject, and come up with a few concepts that I can send for you to look at.

**Tammy Barley:** (Note to reader: This is sometimes difficult to do from an author's perspective. I suggest connecting with a cover artist as soon as your manuscript editor begins his or her work.)

Jim, when an author first contacts you, what information do you need from him in order to begin work? What questions do you ask?

**Jim Saurbaugh:** First question is always, "What is the title?" Then I would need the overall book dimensions. From there I ask a list of questions that will fine-tune the creative process, such as:

- Why did you write this book?
- Who did you write this book for? Who is your audience?
- What do you want the reader to feel when they see the cover?
- Do you have any ideas on a design already?
- Are there any existing book covers you really love? (I don't copy other designs, but I do take inspiration from other books, magazines, Web sites, or anything a client really likes, and try to incorporate that into my design.)

Usually this is about all I need to get started, then after a few rounds of revisions and tweaking, a cover is born.

**Tammy Barley:** How often do authors contribute ideas for the book-cover design, and how often do they rely on you to brainstorm ideas?

**Jim Saurbaugh:** Authors almost always have some thought or idea in mind, even if I have to coax it out of them. Don't be afraid to tell a designer your thoughts, but don't be offended if those thoughts won't make for a successful cover. You may have a great idea a designer might not have thought of, or you might be surprised to learn that seven different fonts, an entire rainbow of colors, and a fourteen-word title doesn't really make an attractive cover.

**Tammy Barley:** You mentioned research. Before you begin to design a book cover, what kinds of research do you do? Research at your client's Web site? Books of similar genre and content as that of your client?

**Jim Saurbaugh:** I research as much as I can. Whatever I don't learn from the initial contact, I gain from their Web site or past published books. Yes, I look at books of similar genre and content. I look at them to see what has been done before, so mine will stand out from the competition. I sometimes will look for inspiration, if it is a subject I might not be able to relate to. I look at them to get a sense of the message they are trying to get across, and to whom it is directed.

**Tammy Barley:** "So mine will stand out from the competition." Undoubtedly you've done that. The cover of every book I've worked with you on absolutely does. They also convey the author's business brand. How do you work with a business-book author to achieve the unique designs he needs in order to mirror his brand and writing style?

**Jim Saurbaugh:** As I mentioned in the question on what questions I ask to begin work, I ask a lot of background questions that seemingly don't have anything to do with design. I try to get a feel for the author as a person in that initial contact. It is almost like a mini interview. I can learn a lot from that about the author. If he/she is funny and light-hearted and so is the book, then the design will reflect that.

Interior graphics are the same way. The inside has to coordinate with the outside. If it doesn't, it is almost like watching a bad movie. "The cover looked like a sci-fi thriller, but it ended up being a musical!"

**Tammy Barley:** For a moment, I'd like to explore a few specific design elements. How do you determine a book title's placement on the front cover? When should the book title occupy the top half of the book cover, and when should the author's name be spotlighted in that space?

**Jim Saurbaugh:** In my experience, the author usually will tell me if they want their name to be the focal point. I think if you are a well-known author (Stephen King or Danielle Steele), your name sells the book for you. If you are new to the scene or relatively obscure, and want people to learn your name over the title, then that is a valid argument. If it ends up being more of an ego trip, then I would say spend a little more effort coming up with a clever title.

**Tammy Barley:** How do you determine what font size a book's title should be?

**Jim Saurbaugh:** Well, my answer is very non-scientific. I base my title font size on what looks good with the image, and the size of the book.

**Tammy Barley:** How many images and fonts do you have in your arsenal?

**Jim Saurbaugh:** I have literally thousands of fonts and images at my fingertips. If my computer doesn't have what I'm looking for, I go out and find it.

I start with free fonts first, to keep cost down, and if that produces no satisfying results, I get the author's permission to purchase a font we both agree on.

Images come from an art service I subscribe to, or in some cases, I create my own original image, depending on the project. Not all subjects coordinate with hand-drawn art.

**Tammy Barley:** What artistic mediums to you specialize in for designing book covers?

**Jim Saurbaugh:** I have only done computer design for covers. I know my strengths and weaknesses, and as much as I love to do traditional art, for me, doing a one-off custom painting for a cover just isn't practical for time or cost.

**Tammy Barley:** How does the dpi resolution of a print-book cover differ from that of an e-book? What dpi do you recommend for each for optimal clarity?

**Jim Saurbaugh:** For print, 300 dpi is the standard. An e-book is lower since the device you use to view it requires that for optimal loading and viewing.

**Tammy Barley:** Your words of wisdom for non-artist authors who might debate using a do-it-yourself book-cover template?

**Jim Saurbaugh:** Templates are the "fast food" answer to design. A template, while convenient and inexpensive, fills a need, but leaves you unimpressed and wishing you had gone with something else. They blend in with all the other people out there who used a template, or worse yet, the same template! That is like two girls showing up at the prom in the same dress!

**Tammy Barley:** Do some book-cover designers use templates? If so, are these artists cutting corners, or do they know how to manipulate the templates in order to achieve pleasing results?

**Jim Saurbaugh:** I would be careful what you pay a designer who uses templates. They may use templates to get a job done faster and charge a custom-design price. A good designer should be able to create a cover on their own. It's all right to look around other designers' work for inspiration, but using templates, in my opinion, is just a cop-out.

**Tammy Barley:** What is the average turnaround time for you to design, from brainstorming phase to finished book cover?

**Jim Saurbaugh:** Two to three weeks is best. It sometimes will go longer than that depending on corrections and design tweaks, but that is usually a good start. Plan ahead! Don't wait until the last minute and then try to crank out a cover. In the end, you might not be happy with it, and you will have boxes and boxes of reminders that you didn't plan ahead.

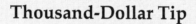

## Thousand-Dollar Tip

"I would be careful what you pay a designer who uses templates. They may use templates to get a job done faster and charge a custom-design price. A good designer should be able to create a cover on their own."

—Jim Saurbaugh

## Interior Graphics

**Tammy Barley:** I'd also like to ask you a few questions about interior graphics. First, when should the author contact you, or another graphic artist, for assistance with interior designs?

**Jim Saurbaugh:** Interior graphics, such as those some people put on chapter beginning pages, should begin when you have the content finalized. This can take a little longer than the cover, in that the artwork should represent what that chapter is about. It would be faster if an author would give a summary of each chapter as opposed to me reading the book all the way through first.

**Tammy Barley:** How often do authors contribute ideas for interior graphics, and how often do they rely on the artist to brainstorm ideas?

**Jim Saurbaugh:** Every time is different. An author may have ideas for the entire book, or just one chapter. Let the artist know your ideas, and they should be able to build from that.

**Tammy Barley:** What artistic mediums are used for designing interior graphics? Pencil? Ink? Computer design? Computer programs you use? How do the artist and client determine which to use?

**Jim Saurbaugh:** For me, mostly computer design. Illustrations are typically done in Adobe Illustrator, and everything else is done with InDesign, Photoshop. If anything is drawn with pencil or ink, I always recreate it in Illustrator to get the best print quality.

**Tammy Barley:** What kinds of interior graphics are available for an author to consider?

**Jim Saurbaugh:** There are literally thousands of stock images to consider, as well as custom-designed graphics that are specific to the information you need to illustrate. The designer can . . . simply create their own, based on the style of the author.

**Tammy Barley:** What is the minimum dpi illustrations should be in order to appear legibly in print books? What dpi do you recommend to achieve optimal clarity? Recommended dpi for photographs?

**Jim Saurbaugh:** Illustrations and photos should be 300 dpi at 100%.

That means a 300-dpi image placed in a book then enlarged 200% doesn't count. As you scale images up in size, the resolution (dpi) decreases. So a 300-dpi image enlarged 200% will actually only be around 150 dpi.

**Tammy Barley:** Dpi for e-book graphics, illustrations, and photos?

**Jim Saurbaugh:** Here I prefer 150 dpi. Mainly because it is always better to scale down than up.

**Tammy Barley:** While we're on the subject of e-books, are more clients requesting color graphics and illustrations for their e-books' interiors, since many e-readers display color? How does this design process differ from the process you use when designing graphics for print books?

**Jim Saurbaugh:** The design process is the same. Resolution and overall size differs, but that is about it.

**Tammy Barley:** Back to print books for a minute. Is any image file too large for self-publishing companies to download?

**Jim Saurbaugh:** It depends. If the publisher has an FTP site, you can upload and download extremely large files. YouSendIt.com is good for e-mailing large files you normally can't send through Yahoo!, Gmail, or Verizon. The publisher receives a link to your file rather than the file itself, then they have fourteen days to retrieve your image.

**Tammy Barley:** What is the average turnaround time for you (or another artist) to design an interior graphic, from brainstorming phase to finished illustration?

**Jim Saurbaugh:** I would say about a week is a comfortable time frame. If there are several graphics to create, then that would adjust accordingly. It does depend on the complexity and quantity of the graphics required.

## Final Questions

**Tammy Barley:** What is your work philosophy as a graphic designer?

**Jim Saurbaugh:** My goal is to see that the client is happy and excited about the look of their project. It makes it a lot easier to promote and sell if you love the way it looks in your hands. I do all that research I mentioned earlier in an effort to keep changes and tweaks to a minimum, but they do happen. Sometimes the first design is tossed and I start over if the client isn't wild about it. In the end, however, my goal is to make sure you love it.

**Tammy Barley:** Every field has its vetted, respected professionals and its bad guys. If your schedule is full, and an author wants to connect with a graphic designer before you have availability, how should he go about locating another reputable artist? What positives should he look for, and what should he steer clear of?

**Jim Saurbaugh:** Ask around. If I cannot direct you to someone I feel comfortable will do a great job, you may know a fellow author who has an artist he/she is willing to share. Using the same artist doesn't mean your covers will look the same . . . that is, unless they use templates.

**Tammy Barley:** Jim, any other questions clients typically ask you about book covers that I haven't thought to ask?

**Jim Saurbaugh:** I mentioned this earlier, but feel it is important enough to repeat. Plan ahead! The more time you can give a designer to create a cover, the better the result will be. It is less stressful for all involved and shows in the final product. Just like in school, a teacher always could tell which science project was done the night before—a mobile of the solar system using only galvanized washers and the planet names written on them with a Sharpie.

**Tammy Barley:** Jim, thank you. Non-artists will benefit from all the inside knowledge you've provided. We're grateful for your contributions to this book.

**Jim Saurbaugh:** Happy to do it, and I thank you for letting me be a part of it.

## About Jim Saurbaugh

Born and raised in Lancaster County, Pennsylvania, I grew up with a passion for art. Always drawing and creating, and my family kept almost everything. I struggled in school, but always felt at home in art class. With the help of my family and a few inspirational teachers, I managed to graduate from McCaskey High School in 1991.

From there I went on to The Pennsylvania School of Art & Design, where I chose Commercial Art as my career path. It is also where I met my beautiful wife of seventeen years. I worked at Lancaster Newspapers for the *Intelligencer Journal* as a paste-up artist, at night while going to school. After making the dean's list, I graduated from PSA&D and got my break to work as a graphic designer during the day, thanks to the retail sales manager at the time.

Married and one child later, I started my own freelance graphic design business in our home. Nothing fancy at first, just enough to pad the bank account. Oh, how it grew. I got another break doing freelance work for a local ad agency, which led to a full-time position. I worked there for thirteen years before the economy went south and I, like so many others, got laid off, Friday, March 11, 2011. Now with three daughters, my wife and I looked at our options, and that weekend began preparing for lean times and the unknown trials and triumphs of being a self-employed freelance artist.

But as they say, when one door closes, another opens, and on Monday, March 14, 2011, I was fortunate enough to start doing freelance work for a prominent local agency. After three short weeks, I was hired full time and work there happily to this day.

I am very lucky to have a supportive wife to help with all the paperwork a home business can generate. I keep the freelance business going with a loyal client base and word-of-mouth references, including work with the Lancaster Relay for Life. My hope is that my daughters will adopt a similar work ethic and be able to flourish in any economy.

When I am not doing art, my hobbies are finding, restoring, and reselling antiques and enjoying sunny days driving my 1966 Oldsmobile Cutlass convertible with my family.

**You can contact Jim Saurbaugh at:**

J.S. Graphic Design
P: 717-341-9504
F: 717-569-6262
jsgd@verizon.net

## A Quick Note to Readers

Graphic artists, like manuscript editors, come in all shades and levels of experience and professionalism, so make sure you bring on board one you can work with long term. Since you might produce another book or two, it will be handy to find one you can easily work with on future projects.

Good graphic artists will work to understand your book and business goals, and will make updates until the art is exactly what you need it to be.

## Begin Creative Artistry

Connect with your graphic artist(s) now, and have him design your cover and interior graphics.

Have your editor proofread all wording used on the front and back book-cover art and the spine, as well as any wording included in the interior graphics.

When all editorial updates have been made and your artist's work is complete, your artist will send you the graphics files. You or your editor can incorporate the interior graphics files into your manuscript document and format each one's size and position for optimal appearance on the page.

For cartoons, add any necessary captions beneath the images. If each cartoon is placed on a page of its own, include a caption to anchor the illustration, so that it does not visually float around the page space.

Note: If you plan to self-publish a paper book or an e-book, you will need to obtain your ISBN and bar code, which can usually be done through the self-publishing company you use. As I noted previously, be sure the ISBN is in your name, not the self-publishing company's name. (Self-publishing will be discussed in Part 5, coming up next.) You can begin that process while your cover designer is creating the artwork. Once you have the ISBN and the bar code file, your cover designer will need to add them to your back cover, or dust jacket if you plan to publish a hardcover book.

Start your creative artistry now. Go ahead. I'll gladly wait.

## One Final Step Before You Prepare to Publish

Now that your book's artwork is underway, you are undoubtedly *jazzed*! Your emotions are flying at Mach 5 (either that or you already passed it). You're twitching with the need to see—to touch, to hold, to show off—your published book. Your baby.

You're one single step away from being ready to publish.

And here it is.

After all of your interior graphics have been added and your editor has completed all of your manuscript's formatting, fill your printer with blank paper, and print out your manuscript. Give it a final read-through, and verify how the text and graphics look on the page. If you see any problems, have your editor or graphic artist make the update(s).

Once the printed version looks great, you'll be ready to publish.

Part 5

# Traditional-, Self-, or E-Publish

Chapter 17

# Publishing Options: Traditional Publishing Houses

## Factors to Consider When Deciding How to Publish

Welcome back! Ready to publish? Then let's get started.

Print books remain favored by many learners, who read with colored highlighters and pens clutched in one eager fist and the empty lines of an open notebook a few inches away. These readers salivate in anticipation of a chunk of wisdom they can highlight, underline, circle, draw arrows next to in the margins, and write down, so they can easily recall and refer to the passage in the future.

However, with the advancements in e-reader and especially interactive tablet technology, nonfiction readers can now highlight and add notes within an e-book they've purchased, and click links for instant, additional information. As this technology becomes even more user-friendly and interactive, it will gain in popularity with business-book consumers.

Today most traditional and self-publishing companies publish their books in both print and e-format, giving consumers flexibility in purchase options.

Or, should you self-publish your book? In paper, e-format, or both? As always, when deciding how to proceed, consider your particular readers, and your goals for the book and for your business.

Chapters 17, 18, and 19 will give you more information to help you decide which publishing option or options—traditional-, self-, and/or e-publishing—will work best for you.

# Pros and Cons of Working with Traditional Publishing Houses

Also called brick-and-mortar publishers, traditional publishers remain the vehicle many writers first think of when they consider how to go about printing and distributing their books. Many writers also believe that the old publishing method depicted in the movie *The Ghost and Mrs. Muir* (Rex Harrison, Gene Tierney) still holds true· I write a book, send it to a publisher, and then relax and collect handsome royalty checks until it's time for my dirt nap.

Unfortunately, changes in business practices and supply and demand within the publishing world made that dream obsolete decades ago. Publishing houses receive hundreds, even thousands, of manuscript submissions every week. They can publish only a small percentage of those, and only those that can potentially generate the highest income for the publisher.

With that in mind, here is the basic process a manuscript and author go through when an author submits it in hopes of publication.

### Literary Agent

Few reputable (trustworthy) publishing houses accept submissions directly from authors. They only accept submissions from literary agents with whom they have an established relationship or whose agency is familiar to them, since literary agents essentially vet manuscripts and authors for them.

So, the author must find and contract with a literary agent who 1) believes in the author's work and its ability to generate income for the literary agency as well as a publishing house, 2) has the scheduling availability to be able to field the manuscript on behalf of the author, and 3) has contacts at publishing houses who are currently seeking the genre and subject matter of the manuscript in question.

Few literary agents possess #3. Instead, they contract with an author for a promising manuscript and hope some publishing house will soon seek out that particular manuscript's genre and subject matter and then contract for the manuscript. It's what's needed in order for literary agencies to remain in business so that they can continue to help authors publish their books. However, an author should try to contract with a literary agent who already has contact with a publisher who is actively seeking their manuscript's genre and subject matter (a rare find, unfortunately), or else the manuscript can remain locked in contract with a literary agent who is not currently able to benefit the author. Oftentimes, this is the best literary agents can do, and a percentage of the books they contract for do eventually sell to publishing houses.

With the explosion of self-publishing options, and thus the decline of publishing houses, the direction and future of literary agents and agencies is uncertain, but many continue to provide this service both for authors and publishing houses.

In order to find a literary agent who represents your genre and subject matter, reference Writer's Digest's (www.WritersDigest.com) annual *Guide to Literary Agents* and www.LiteraryMarketPlace.com.

Or, if you have found books similar to yours, go to each publisher's Web site, find their Submission Guidelines, and see if they work solely with literary agents or if the publisher accepts submissions straight from authors.

In order to submit to a literary agent (or publisher), you will need to send, based on each literary agent's (or publisher's) particular requirements, a query letter and possibly a synopsis, proposal, and pages or chapters of your manuscript.

Each of these documents—query letter, synopsis, and proposal—requires precise elements and formatting, each of which takes months of time to develop and perfect—another reason to work with a manuscript editor who is already a published author and possesses this expertise.

All of this takes several days, often weeks, to carry out, in order to begin contacting literary agents.

A word of caution regarding how literary agents and traditional publishers process manuscript submissions.

Literary agents and publishing houses' acquisitions editors do one thing, hour after hour, every day: read manuscript submissions. Speaking as a former acquisitions editor, all of that reading gets hard on the eyes, until one's eyes feel like they've been hung out to dry in a hot desert wind. Words blur, lines blur, and unusual fonts and weird formatting distract the reader from the content. So, industry professionals have developed a standard manuscript format that is easy to read, and easy for the author to implement.

Now here is the word of caution: Agents and acquisitions editors people have dozens, sometimes hundreds, of manuscript submissions sitting on their desks or in their e-mail inboxes at all times. As agents and acquisitions editors skim and reject twenty submissions, twenty more arrive. The stack never goes down. So they skim each submission within a few minutes. They are not looking for reasons to contract for each manuscript, but reasons to reject it so they get back to hopefully, prayerfully, whittling down the pile. Manuscripts that land on literary agents' and publishers' desks that are not formatted according to industry standards receive a heavy strike against them, and many manuscripts never make it past this initial glance before they are declined.

To agents and acquisitions editors, incorrect manuscript formatting (and incorrect query letter, synopsis, and proposal content and formatting) suggests a lack of respect for the recipient, and also indicates an inexperienced author, or one who lacks professionalism and who would be difficult—too difficult—to work with.

Special note #1: Books with word counts that exceed 100,000 are financially unfeasible to publish. The more the words, the higher the cost to produce, and the less the profit for the publisher. Publishing houses can rarely consider books with word counts above 100K.

Special note #2: Publishers look for authors who will produce multiple books each, rather than multiple authors who will produce only one book each. Doing so is simply more time- and cost-effective. It would negatively affect their business to do otherwise.

One other word of caution: If a literary agent wants to charge you to read your manuscript, you'll need to decide whether the fee is reasonable, or whether the agent is making false promises about the future of the manuscript in hopes of raking in additional income from "editing" and other services they can provide, each for yet another fee. If you determine the latter, and the agent doesn't have a verifiable record of selling books like yours to reputable publishers, *run* the other direction. Some so-called agents charge a reading fee then pay students to provide a critique for them. They make their income this way, not from helping writers to publish.

Again, a manuscript editor who is also a published author will be able to assist you with virtually all the above details and lift their related concerns from you.

To research publishers who might accept manuscript submissions directly from authors, consult the Writer's Digest annual *Writer's Market*.

**Warning:** Not all literary agents or publishers are good guys. In fact, many are not. To determine if a particular agent or publisher has a positive record or a negative one, find him in the Predators & Editors listings at www.Pred-Ed.com.

## On to the Publishing House

If you have contracted with a literary agent, and he submits your manuscript to a publishing house's acquisitions editor, here are the next steps in the process.

The acquisitions editor (we'll call him AE, for simplicity) will need, or take, anywhere from a week to as much as six months to initially glance at your manuscript submission. If the manuscript matches what the AE is seeking, if you have an established platform from which to sell several thousand copies of the book, if you have a marketing plan in place to do exactly that, and if you are currently at work on your next manuscript(s), then he will consider the submission further.

The reason why you need a platform and marketing plan is because the lion's share of publishing-house budgets goes to promote their best-selling authors—their proven income-generators. Comparatively little money is designated to invest in promotion of an unknown author. You must promote your book yourself in order to be sure potential buyers will hear about it.

If your manuscript concept, development, and writing are excellent, and the AE believes it has solid potential for a high number of sales, the AE will send the manuscript on to a committee. The committee determines whether or not to contract for each proposed manuscript. Committee members must each read *every* proposed manuscript. Publishing houses differ in how often the committee meets to vote. Some meet only twice per year.

As you can see, traditional publishing can be a very long process.

If the committee votes to offer a contract for a manuscript, the contract is drawn up, sent to the literary agent who deciphers any intellectual property legalese you might be unfamiliar with, then the contract is signed by both parties. With it, an advance is offered and agreed upon, usually a small one. The advance is an advance royalty payment, not a purchase sum. You do not receive additional royalty payments until the advance has been paid for by book sales.

The publishing house sets a date for publication roughly six months out, sometimes a year or longer (many work on an eighteen-month production cycle), then the manuscript is sent to the editorial department. There, an editor is assigned to work with you to do rewrites. Once the manuscript rewrites fit the publishing house's vision of the future book, the manuscript goes through other processes, including a new book title (sometimes), and book-cover design and interior layouts, which the author typically has little say in.

So, the publishing house takes care of, or assists you with, all the above details, prints your manuscript, gets your book on bookstore shelves (and often makes the electronic version available), and helps to promote your book, to some degree or other.

Your royalties will usually be, for soft-cover books, between 6.5 percent and 10 percent of the cover price. So if your book sells for, say $14 (the publisher determines the cover price), your royalties will be between 91 cents and $1.40 per book. (Of that, approximately 15 percent is paid to your literary agent for his work.) The balance reimburses the expenses the publishing house has incurred, because they have invested in the technology and manpower to publish, distribute, and market your book, and because they assume the financial risk of its success. Their net remains are profits.

After promotion and sales of your first book are underway, the publisher will want your next manuscript. The more books that your name appears on, the more you will get noticed and talked about. Then everyone benefits, including your business and its team as well as the publishing house. If you fail to keep pace with the schedule that the publisher expects, they will not want to publish your future books, and will not do so after the contract terms have been met.

That is the basic process of working with a traditional publisher. If you are willing to invest the time and take the steps to contract with a publishing house and give over a lot of the detail work to them, and if this will best benefit you and your goals, (and if your subject matter won't be old news if/when it finally publishes), then traditional publishing may be an option for you. However, working with a publishing house that produces multiple genres is *not* a method I recommend.

If you want to work with a publishing house, then I recommend that those of you who are B2B entrepreneurs and info marketers connect with a publisher that specializes in business books similar to yours. Business-book publishers will be more attuned to your needs, your audience, and have more targeted means of book promotion.

How do you find traditional publishers that work with books like yours? Well, remember the Competitor Book Research Sheets you filled out while researching your competitors in Chapter 2? The names of prospective publishers are right there. Visit those publishers' Web sites to see whether they will accept manuscript submissions directly from authors.

Self-publishing, in comparison, is a very fast process, your book is guaranteed to publish, you will have control over all details related to your book, you can own the rights to your book from day one, and self-publishing pays approximately 50 percent of the cover price in royalties. You will need to market your book whether it is traditionally or self-published.

The final significant difference between traditional and self-publishing is that self-publishing does *not* guarantee your book will appear on bookstore shelves. This might not be a factor for you, if you do not need bookstore distribution, or if you get your books onto bookstore shelves yourself.

Is traditional publishing the best way to explode your business's profits?

Due to the myriad disadvantages to authors, traditional publishing has lost its appeal for most writers. However, some business-book writers still work with publishers that specialize in that genre.

Next up—the pros and cons of working with a self-publishing company.

# Chapter 18

# Publishing Options: Self-Publishing Companies

## Pros and Cons of Working with Self-Publishing Companies

I'll keep this simple, since working with self-publishing companies is fairly simple.

**Pros:**

- It's a quick process—you can be holding published copies in a matter of days.
- Your book is guaranteed to publish.
- You'll have control over all details related to your book, including book title, cover design, interior graphics and layout, and of course, the way the content is written.
- You can own the rights to your book from day one.
- Most self-publishing companies see to your book's ISBN, bar code, and similar book-related requirements for you.
- Self-publishing pays approximately 50 percent of the cover price in royalties (varies among self-publishing companies).

## Cons:

- You'll have control over all details related to your book, including book title, cover design, interior graphics and layout, and of course, the way the content is written.

  Why I list this as a con for you to consider is because you'll be the project coordinator, which will require a moderate investment of your time.

  If you don't have time to coordinate your project, you can instead hire a manuscript coordinator to quarterback your project for you. Some manuscript editors have this expertise.

- Your book does not necessarily end up on bookstore shelves. This might not be a factor for you, if you do not need bookstore distribution.

  If you want them in bookstores, you must learn how to do this yourself, or hire an experienced promoter to pitch your book to book buyers for you.

- Self-publishing requires a financial investment to publish the books, usually quite modest, and you receive no advance on royalties. To many business-book authors, the months, sometimes years, saved in self-publishing versus traditional publishing makes up for the expenditure many times over.

Not all self-publishing companies are good guys. In fact, many are not. So how do you know which self-publishing company to work with?

Answer: Simple. Pick up a copy of *The Fine Print of Self-Publishing, Everything You Need to Know About the Costs, Contracts & Process of Self-Publishing*, Fourth Edition, by Mark Levine, attorney and CEO of Hillcrest Media Group, Inc. Just as you can't complete your manuscript effectively without the assistance of an editor, or produce a captivating book cover and interior art without a graphic artist, you cannot self-publish effectively without knowing the information in this short, easy-to-read book.

Actually, the book content is about 265 pages, but I call it "short and easy to read" because you want the best self-publishing company for your book, so you only need to read the first 141 pages or so. The reason is that the author, Mark Levine, provides need-to-know information at the beginning of the book, such as understanding the fine print in self-publishing contracts, then follows it with a breakdown of "Outstanding Self-Publishers" and "Pretty Good Self-Publishers," which is all you need. The rest of the book details "Publishers Who Are Just Okay" and "Publishers to Avoid."

Levine's book includes URLs to all the self-publishing companies he evaluates, and what you have to know about each company.

Most self-publishing companies use Lightning Source (www1.LightningSource.com) to print books on demand, and to sell them via www.Amazon.com and www.BarnesAndNoble.com. This means their printing costs are identical. What they tell you their printing costs are, not surprisingly, are not identical.

Also, Advantage Media Group (www.gkicpublishing.com) has fee-based publishing and marketing services available, if you want it done for you.

Several self-publishing companies also offer e-publishing services.

Feel like you need a publisher's name on your self-published book to give it added credibility? True, "Self-Published by ___" doesn't impress. Then simply develop a business name to publish your books and related materials under (that's how Business Book Productions originated), and then your publishing mode conveys the same solidarity and professionalism as the rest of your business.

Check and abide by applicable laws, if any. You might be required to file your publisher name with your city or your county as a fictitious business name, and possibly post a DBA (Doing-Business-As) notice in your local newspaper. (More information about that in Chapter 23.) While your book is in the process of being published, set up a Web site under your publishing name to advertise your books and similar materials.

With all considerations, self-publishing provides greater opportunities to explode your business profits, sooner, than trying to work with most brick-and-mortar publishers.

Chapter 19

# Publishing Options: E-Publishing

## Will E-Book Popularity Cause Decreases in Demand for Print Books in the Next Five Years?

Industry gurus continue to speculate what the next five years will bring about in the world of publishing. Their forecasts are educated guesses, and many of them caution that no one can know the future of publishing beyond a doubt, because the technological changes now taking place are unprecedented. Here is what we do know.

According to BookStats ("The Center for Publishing Market Data"), United States publishers' net e-book sales revenue has increased more than 1000 (yes, one thousand) percent in just three years, from 2008 to 2010.

Note that the above and the following statistics do not distinguish between genres, such as fiction and nonfiction. E-fiction typically outsells e-nonfiction (specifically, business books) at the present, yet the statistics are hard to ignore.

The Association of American Publishers notes that in 2010, print-book sales changed little from print book sales in 2009. Thus, according to AAP, the popularity of p-books (print books) currently remains fairly constant, even amid skyrocketing enthusiasm for e-books.

However, a recent study conducted by The Book Industry Study Group, Inc. (BISG) reveals that the scales are beginning to tip in favor of e-books. Of all book readers who participated in the survey, two-thirds report they have moved either mostly or exclusively from print to e-books.

**Rapid Growth in Demand for English-Language Books Worldwide**

Here are a few more eye-opening statistics.

In May 2012, the Association of American Publishers released a report that showed US publishers of various genres, including nonfiction, noted *worldwide* sales increases in English-language p- and e-books in 2010 and 2011. Reasons include greater Internet access to books published in the United States.

Outside of the United States, more than 750 million people around the globe read English. Currently US publishers export an average of 90% of their p- and/or e-books to distributors in 200 countries.

Rapid-growth regions include:

- **UK**—more than 1315% gain year to year (2010, 2011) in e-book purchases, more than 10% increase in p-book purchases
- **Africa**—more than 635% increase in e-books, 17% plus in p-books
- **Continental Europe**—more than 215% e-book gains, 9.5% increases in the print versions
- **Latin America**—200% more e-books purchased, and nearly 10% more print books

Publishers project that this growth pattern will continue for the foreseeable future.

# Pros and Cons of E-Publishing

## Pros:

- The author has control over virtually every aspect of the book (as with self-publishing p-books).
- Little up-front cost, usually to purchase the ISBN and bar code. Free file upload with many e-publishers, which means zero cost to produce.
- It's fast—you can be selling copies within two days.
- Sell with no fulfillment costs or effort on your part. Buyers download the e-book themselves at the e-publisher's Web site.
- E-books can be any length.
- Multimedia capability—such as sound, color images, graphics with motion, hyperlinks.
- Readership may become greater than that of p-books, depending on your audience.

   Consumers love having a pocket-sized library of information, plus e-books are typically priced a few dollars lower than p-books.

- E-books never go out of print, so you can keep profiting, even after you retire, as long as your book remains in demand.
- Paperless mass production.


## Cons:

- Typically little income through book sales (often lower than self-publishing p-books), though remember: *Book sales won't make you money; you'll make money because the book sells you.*
- No universal catalogues of available titles.
- Your audience might not be predominantly e-book readers.
- Some books sell well, others don't.
- Currently, e-book vendors lack a set, standard format.
- E-book quality fluctuates between great and mediocre.

## Should You E-Publish?

If your audience reads e-books, then yes, publish in e-book format, and e-publish your book yourself. I'll show you how in Chapter 22.

It costs brick-and-mortar publishing houses little to e-publish your book, yet they pocket most of the earnings, and pass a miniscule percentage of the royalties down to you. Also, due to contract language, as long as your e-books are selling, these profit rights can remain with the publishing house virtually indefinitely.

E-publish yourself, and the resulting net sales profits and rights can be yours alone, as they should be.

## My Publishing Recommendation

Since anyone can publish an e-book—and tens of thousands of folks do, often with poor quality of content—e-books do *not* give a business author the same cachet that he gains from publishing a p-book. You must publish a p-book to be seen as an authority.

What's great about this is, when your p-book manuscript is ready to publish, so is your e-book. If you opt to convert it to an a-book (audio book), the script for it is already done as well.

So, unless a dedicated business-book publisher would best meet your needs, you should self-publish a p-book *and* e-publish, if your audience contains dedicated e-book readers.

Both book forms are juicy bait which can lure presold prospects into your business and explode your profits!

## A Quick Note about the Next Three Chapters

Chapter 20 will teach you how to submit your manuscript to a brick-and-mortar publisher.

Chapter 21 will show you how to work with a self-publishing company.

Chapter 22 is all about e-publishing.

Feel free to read only the chapter(s) that applies to you.

## Chapter 20

# How to Format Your Manuscript for Traditional Publication

Format, as I use the word here, means how the text appears on the page. If you plan to submit your manuscript for publication to a literary agent and/or a traditional brick-and-mortar publisher, your manuscript will need to be formatted for submission according to publishing industry standards.

A quick reminder from Chapter 17: Manuscripts that land on literary agents' and publishers' desks that are not formatted according to industry standards receive a heavy strike against them—and many manuscripts never make it past this initial glance before they are declined.

So, what font should you use for text? Where should the text on the first page of each chapter start? Where should the page numbers go? How wide should the margins be? What information appears in the top margins of each page?

If you have questions about formatting, the answers are here.

If you work with a manuscript editor, he or she can perform virtually all of the following for you, though it's important to be familiar with the information in this chapter so that you understand how various processes work and what to expect from your editor.

## Manuscript Format for Submission to a Literary Agent or Traditional Publisher

Formatting involves several steps, but they're all simple.

1. Your manuscript should be saved in a .doc or .docx electronic file format
2. One inch margins on all sides
3. All lines double spaced
4. No blank lines before or after paragraphs

Here is what it looks like:

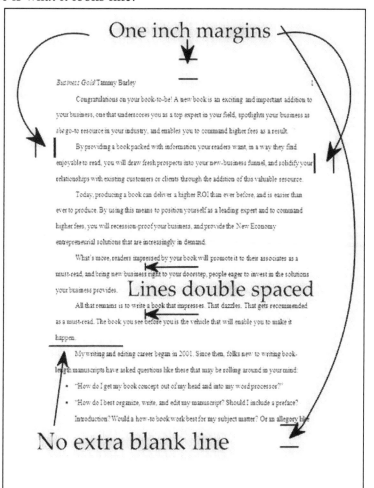

5. All text Times New Roman 12-point font
6. Only one space between sentences
7. Half-inch paragraph indents

Here are what they look like:

8. Left margin justified only (ragged right margin)
9. Page number in upper right corner
10. Page header in upper left corner: Book title/your name in Times New Roman 12-point font

Page header

*Business Gold*/Tammy Barley   Page number here⟨ 1 ⟩

Congratulations on your book-to-be! A new book is an exciting and important addition to your business, one that underscores you as a top expert in your field, spotlights your business as *the* go-to resource in your industry, and enables you to command higher fees as a result.

By providing a book packed with information your readers want, in a way they find enjoyable to read, you will draw fresh prospects into your new-business funnel, and solidify your relationships with existing customers or clients through the addition of this valuable resource.

Today, producing a book can deliver a higher ROI than ever before, and is easier than ever to produce. By using this means to position yourself as a leading expert and to command higher fees, you will recession-proof your business, and provide the New Economy entrepreneurial solutions that are increasingly in demand.

What's more, readers impressed by your book will promote it to their associates as a must-read, and bring new business right to your doorstep, people eager to invest in the solutions your business provides.

All that remains is to write a book that impresses. That dazzles. That gets recommended as a must-read. The book you see before you is the vehicle that will enable you to make it happen.

My writing and editing career began in 2001. Since then, folks new to writing book-length manuscripts have asked questions like these that may be rolling around in your mind:

- "How do I get my book concept out of my head and into my word processor?"
- "How do I best organize, write, and edit my manuscript? Should I include a preface? Introduction? Would a how-to book work best for my subject matter? Or an allegory like

Justified left margin

Ragged right margin

The first page of each chapter gets its own unique formatting:
1. Six blank lines (double spaced)
2. On line seven, insert the chapter number, spelled out (Times New Roman 12-point font), centered
3. On line eight, insert the chapter title (Times New Roman 12-point font), centered
4. Line nine is blank
5. On line ten, begin text

Like this:

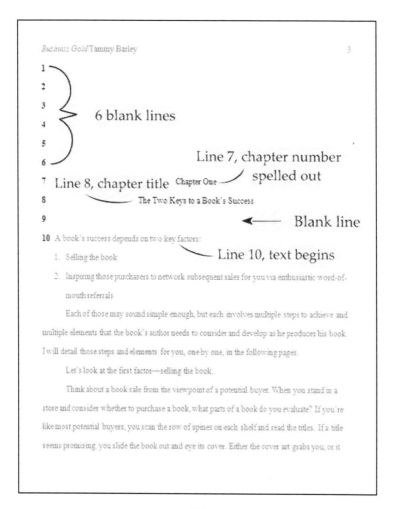

Of course, you would not insert any line numbers in your document.

To insert a section header, place it flush left, bolded:

*Business Gold/*Tammy Barley       1

Today, producing a book can deliver a higher ROI than ever before, and is easier than ever to produce. By using this means to position yourself as a leading expert and to command higher fees, you will recession-proof your business, and provide the New Economy entrepreneurial solutions that are increasingly in demand.

What's more, readers impressed by your book will promote it to their associates as a must-read, and bring new business right to your doorstep, people eager to invest in the solutions your business provides.

All that remains is to write a book that impresses. That dazzles. That gets recommended as a must-read. The book you see before you is the vehicle that will enable you to make it happen.

$\longleftarrow$ **Blank line** $\longrightarrow$

**My Writing and Editing Career**

My writing and editing career began in 2001. Since then, folks new to writing book-length manuscripts have asked questions like these that may be rolling around in your mind:

1 "How do I get my book concept out of my head and into my word processor?"

2 "How do I best organize, write, and edit my manuscript? Should I include a preface? Introduction? Would a how-to book work best for my subject matter? Or an allegory like *Who Moved My Cheese?* or *The One Minute Manager?* How do I hook a potential reader with the back cover copy?"

**Flush left, bolded**

# Writing and Formatting a Query Letter, Synopsis, and Proposal

One other quick reminder from Chapter 17.

In order to submit to a literary agent, you will need to send, based on each literary agent's particular requirements, a query letter and possibly a synopsis, and/or proposal, in addition to pages or chapters of your manuscript.

Each of these documents—query letter, synopsis, and proposal—requires precise elements and formatting, each of which takes months of time to develop and perfect. You can simply work with a manuscript editor who is already a published author and possesses this expertise.

Due to the time needed to learn and perfect each of these, I do not recommend doing these yourself.

If you're the ultimate do-it-yourselfer and want to write these documents personally, pick up a copy of the most recent edition of *Writer's Market*, published by Writer's Digest Books (available in many libraries). Also research their Web site for any additional information you need: www.WritersDigest.com.

Chapter 21

# How to Self-Publish
# Your P-Book

As I noted several pages ago, if you self-publish, there is one book you can't do without: *The Fine Print of Self-Publishing, Everything You Need to Know About the Costs, Contracts & Process of Self-Publishing*, Fourth Edition, by Mark Levine, attorney and CEO of Hillcrest Media Group, Inc. Authors cannot self-publish safely without knowing the information in this book.

Levine teaches you the fine print you need to be aware of before signing any self-publishing company's contract—including honest and dishonest ways various companies price their "costs" in order to reduce your royalties and augment their profits. Plus he shares everything else you need to know about working with each self-publishing company that he reviews.

He rates the best (most honorable and reputable) self-publishing companies, based on multiple points of information gained while posing as a potential client.

**Those he rates as Outstanding Are:**
Aventine Press
BookLocker

BookPros
Dog Ear Publishing
Infinity Publishing
Tate Publishing
Wasteland Press
Xulon Press
I understand he maintains high standards at his publishing company as well: Hillcrest Media Group, Inc.

**Those he rates as Pretty Good are:**
CreateSpace (Amazon)
Outskirts Press

All the others are categorized as "Publishers Who Are Just Okay," "Publishers to Avoid," or "The Worst of the Worst."

As Levine's book will show you, most decent self-publishing companies offer fairly comparable packages. Many include:

- **soft- and hardcover options, e-book publishing** (Not all self-publishing companies e-publish; some don't publish hardcover)
- **three choices of trim size** (dimensions of published book)
- **ISBN** (Your graphic artist can add this to your back cover)
- **"Bookland EAN bar code/13 with add on"** (Your graphic artist can add this to your back cover)
- **Library of Congress Control Number (LCCN)** (Your editor can add this information to your copyright page; only needed if you want libraries to carry your book)
- **cover design assistance** (Warning: Many of these designers use templates)
- **choice of interior layout templates or formatting of graphics** (Your editor has probably done this for you)
- **printed proof copy for you to review**
- **a couple of free copies of your book**

- **listing of your book with major online booksellers like Amazon.com, BarnesAndNoble.com**
- **submission of your book to Amazon.com's Look Inside!** (If your self-publishing company doesn't offer this option, do it yourself at Amazon.com. Would *you* want to buy a book you couldn't read more about?)
- **book and author Web page at their Web site**
- **submission to book distributor database(s), catalog listing(s), and/or distribution through Ingram or Baker & Taylor**
- **press release writing** (Offered by a few; your editor might assist with this or is likely associated with someone who does; or simply visit www.GebbieInc.com/howto.htm to learn how)
- **registration with the U.S. Copyright Office**

So, most self-publishing companies offer similar services as their competitors. That means the primary differences between them are their contracts, the fees they charge, and the quality of services, including customer service, that they provide.

A few of them advertise book-marketing packages, and can assist with marketing, to one extent or another. Since few to none of the self-publishing companies Levine rated works exclusively with business-book authors, or have any specialty, I suggest weighing their offers carefully. Business-book authors know their audiences well, and can achieve greater success by simply marketing their books themselves or through one or more members of their team.

Another option? Bring on board a book-marketing group that specializes in the business-book genre. In Chapter 26, I'll show you how to connect with the best.

Much like traditional brick-and-mortar publishers, some self-publishing companies are very selective about the manuscripts they will agree to publish, since most of their earnings come from books sold rather than from author purchases of their printing packages. Also, some publish only fiction, or cookbooks, or select nonfiction, and might not publish your genre. Levine's book tells you all of that, and a lot more.

Several of my clients, colleagues, and myself have published through CreateSpace (Amazon), and are consistently delighted with the speed and ease at which they could upload and publish their books, and were equally delighted with CreateSpace's customer service.

Of course, Amazon didn't become Amazon by offering poor products or services.

Also, most self-publishing companies charge for their services. CreateSpace does not. As of this printing, CreateSpace also obtains your ISBN for you at no additional charge, or a "Custom ISBN" for $10, and registers it with BooksInPrint.com®. (For details, see https://www.createspace.com/Products/Book/ISBNs.jsp.) All you have to do is click a button or two. CreateSpace *also* obtains and adds the bar code to the lower right corner of the book's back cover for you, free of charge. I'll note here that the bar code space is 2" wide and 1.2" tall, so your cover designer can plan around it, if you opt to use CreateSpace.

Levine's book includes each self-publishing company's URL, so all you need to do is type it into your browser and follow the instructions at the publisher's Web site.

Be sure to pick up the most recent edition, so that you have his most up-to-date ratings and information.

## Soft Cover, Hardcover, or Both?

Soft cover, definitely. Soft cover is the most familiar to readers, plus it feels comfortable to hold and manipulate.

Hardcover if libraries want to carry your book and if they prefer hardcover form. Ask your local librarians.

Also, hardcover for a subsequent edition if your first edition(s) sell hundreds of thousands of copies. Hardcover feels more formal, but can add prestige and is more durable than soft cover, so it works well for books that are frequently referenced over long periods of time.

## Trim Size

Trim size is simply the height and width of your published page size.

Common trim sizes are 5.5" x 8.5" and 6" x 9". This book is 6" x 9". Sizes can also be smaller or larger. Your self-publishing company will tell you the size options available through them. The choice of trim size is yours entirely.

Considerations when deciding trim size?

- **Page count**—Page counts are commonly 150 to 300 pages, but can be fewer or more. If you have fewer than 100 pages, go with a smaller trim size so that you reduce your current number of words per page, and increase the number of pages in the book. Fewer than 100 pages will result in a narrow spine (about one quarter of an inch), and therefore a small font size for the title on the spine.

  Also, narrow informational/how-to books and business biographies appear to the reader to be slim on content. Allegories easily get away with fewer pages, because readers expect each to convey only one main topic.

  Does your book have 700, 800, or 900 pages? Go with a larger trim size to reduce your page count, or no one will be able to print it in soft cover. Or, divide your manuscript into two or three books. (Then consider a second career as a writer.)

- **Book style**—Did you write an allegory? Allegories are traditionally small to medium sized—5" x 8" to 5.5" x 8.5". Informational/how-to books and business biographies are typically larger—5.5" x 8.5" and 6" x 9".

- **Your goals for the book**—Do you plan for your book to be used as a workbook where readers will be instructed to write on the page? If so, you might want a larger trim size, perhaps as large as 8" x 10".

  A pocket guide? Then go smaller—5" x 8".

  Do you want to convey prestige? Then you don't want it to look like a workbook or a pocket guide, and you want it to stand out among the many 5.5" x 8.5" books, so go with 6" x 9".

- **Cost**—Hardcover books cost more to produce, and therefore must sell at a higher price. However, if the cost difference between soft and hardcover and various trim sizes is relatively minor, this might not be a significant factor for you.

- **Libraries**—Is it likely that libraries will carry your book? Ask your local librarians. If they feel there would be a strong interest for your book in public libraries nationwide, then ask what trim size they would prefer (and whether they would prefer soft- or hardcover).

Once you have decided your trim size, your editor will be able to format your manuscript to fit those dimensions.

# Manuscript Format for Submission to a Self-Publishing Company

The way you format your manuscript pages for self-publishing in your word-processing document is exactly the way the book pages will appear when published. Your manuscript editor should be able to do all of the following for you:

- Your manuscript should be saved in PDF or the electronic file format your self-publishing company specifies.

- Update the manuscript document to the trim size you have chosen.

- Margins should be .5" to .75".

- Add a gutter, if needed. A gutter is a slightly widened margin where the page edges are bound at the spine.

  Not all books have gutters. Gutters are added in thicker books to shift the text fractions of an inch outward from the binding so that the text along the inner margin can be easily read. Your self-publishing company should have a chart that tells how wide of a gutter per how many pages.

- Text is commonly Times New Roman 12-point font, 1.15" line space, no blank line spaces after paragraphs.

  Chapter headers and topic and subtopic header font styles and sizes can vary, though header fonts are typically sans serif.

- IF YOU OPT TO BEGIN each chapter with a decorative initial (a drop capital *or* a raised initial (I began this bulleted point with a raised initial)), then follow it with five or six words in small capitals (LIKE THIS).

- Format position of chapter headers on the page for optimal visual appeal.

- Only one space between sentences.

- Paragraph indents .25".

- Text full justified.

  Occasionally books are left-justified, which can sometimes make for easier reading, but tend to have less of a professional feel.

  Your manuscript is already packed with short paragraphs that keep the reader engaged, so it's already easy on the eyes to read. Go with full justified.

- Add running headers at the tops of the pages—book title or unit title verso (on the left-hand page), and chapter title recto (on the right-hand page). To my chapter titles, I added my chapter numbers, since I refer to my various chapter numbers throughout the book, and so I wanted the chapters to be easy for you to follow.

Running headers never appear on display pages (title page, copyright page, dedication, or epigraph pages) or on the beginning page of other front matter, such as the contents page, foreword, preface, acknowledgments, or introduction/a letter to the reader pages. Typically, no running header on the about-the-author page.

- Add page numbers. I suggest locating these at the bottom of the page, either centered or outside corners, unless your book contains a lot of footnotes.

  Running headers coupled with page numbers all at the top of the page tends to be visually unbalanced and can distract the reader.

- Traditionally, the first page of each chapter begins recto, on the right-hand page. However, if you wish to reduce your book's page count, and the previous chapter ends on a right-hand page, you can begin the next chapter on the verso, the left-hand page. It is your book. When structuring, do what works best to achieve your goals for the book and its readers.

To give you a frame of reference, in the *Business Gold* p-book:
- ✓ Trim size is 6" x 9"
- ✓ Margins are, top and bottom: .75", left and right: .4"
- ✓ Gutter, for this 340(ish)-page book, is: .45"
- ✓ Text is Times New Roman 12-point font, 1.15" line space (no extra space after paragraphs)
- ✓ Chapter numbers are Palatino Linotype 14-point font, bold
- ✓ Chapter titles are Palatino Linotype 20-point font, bold
- ✓ Section headers are Ariel 14-point font, bold
- ✓ Subsection headers Times New Roman 12-point font, bold
- ✓ Only one space between sentences
- ✓ Paragraph indents are .25"
- ✓ Text is full justified

✓ Word count is about 72K

If your book, when printed, will be thin—fewer than 100 pages—and you feel you must add pages, consider using one or more of these:

- Select a smaller trim size for your book
- Format your manuscript using slightly wider margins
- Add a blank line space after each paragraph
- Increase your font size one point
- Add end-of chapter summaries or action steps, or
- Add and end-of-unit summary, or
- Add end-of-book summary
- Add a few blank pages (no more than four) to the back of the book

If your book, when printed, will be thick—more than 400 pages—and seems too exhaustive a volume to attract a reader who wants great information fast, you might opt to decrease the page count. Try one or more of these:

- Select a larger trim size for your book
- Format your manuscript using slightly smaller margins
- Decrease your font size one point
- Avoid end-of-chapter, -unit, and -book summaries
- Ask your editor to tighten (delete unnecessary) content
- Instead of producing one book, divide it and publish two

## Binding and Paper Choices

Most soft-cover books have the cover glued on at the spine. This is called **perfect binding**. It delivers the most professional look to nonfiction soft-cover books. Since other binding choices for soft-cover books look less professional, I don't recommend them.

If you plan to publish your book in hardcover, your self-publishing company will confer with you about the binding choices they offer and what they recommend for your book.

Most common **paper choices**?

- Most common is uncoated book stock—pages look good and photos look fine.
- Less common, mostly due to cost, is coated book stock, either gloss or matte—pages look great and photos look great, so if you print a lot of photos in your book, this may work best for you.

**Paper weight**? A common paper weight for books is 50- to 60-pound stock. A lighter paper weight can look cheap, and also the print from the flipside can ghost through. Heavier paper can make for a stiff page that's hard to turn. I suggest 60-pound stock, which is the paper weight of this page.

**Paper color**? White. It's clean and professional. Cream-colored is best used for novels (fiction).

**Dust jackets** for hardcover books are commonly 80- or 100-pound weight.

# How to Price Your Book

Remember the Competitor Book Research Sheets you filled out in Chapter 2? Use them to determine the best price for your book.

Keep in mind that older books (check the copyright year) will be priced differently than books published in the past few years.

Price your book similar to the recently published books whose page counts are closest to yours. End your price with .95. Why? Ending with .99 sounds pricier, and ending with anything else, such as .49, seems just plain odd.

A warning about under-pricing your book: Under-pricing suggests to a potential buyer that the book lacks quality, or else you'd charge more.

A warning about overpricing your book: If your book costs more than others like yours that have already been published and have received positive reviews, why would anyone want to pay more? Great cover art will help to sell a book, but not if it is unreasonably priced.

## Ready to Publish?

Once you've researched and chosen the self-publishing company you will work with, simply follow the steps at their Web site to begin the publishing process for your manuscript.

After you receive your book's ISBN, bar code, and determine the book's price, have your cover artist add them to the back-cover art or dust jacket art, if you're publishing a hardcover edition.

If you want your book able to be distributed to libraries, then you'll need to obtain an LCCN for your book. Once you have it, your editor can add the LCCN information to the copyright page.

Then your manuscript will be ready to upload to your self-publishing company.

Happy publishing!

Chapter 22

# How to E-Publish

Your p-book is now in the process of being published—congratulations! This means you have, in your possession, a valuable commodity. No, by that I'm not referring to copies of your p-book.

The commodity I'm referring to is your manuscript.

Used in one format, to hook paper-book readers, your manuscript is a powerful asset. Now, use the same manuscript again—to net e-book readers.

Your core audience might not be e-book readers, or they might not be e-book readers today, but at least a smattering of your audience is likely to prefer e-format, and if not today, soon.

If your book isn't available in electronic format, you'll lose potential sales . . . and prospects.

Unless you know for a fact that your target prospect has zero interest in reading nonfiction e-books, I recommend publishing in both p- and e-book formats. The paper version will give you credibility as an expert. The electronic version will make you accessible to prospects who prefer that reading method.

So. You have a brilliantly written, edited, and designed manuscript, and you have the electronic file of your book cover that your artist provided. Where do you publish the e-book?

# E-Publishing Options

Current research indicates that *fiction* readers tend to prefer e-reader devices such as the NOOK and Kindle, but that *nonfiction* readers want the added benefit of interactive multimedia options, and so tend to prefer tablets like the iPad.

What does this mean for your e-book? Simply this: It needs to be available in various e-formats so that it is downloadable to various reader and tablet devices.

### Kindle Direct Publishing

One e-book publisher that many authors consider (and use) is Amazon's Kindle Direct Publishing (www.KDP.Amazon.com). Publishing with KDP is free, and the Amazon reputation stands behind the product and service.

From their Web site: "With Kindle Direct Publishing (KDP) you can self-publish your books on the Amazon Kindle Store. It's free, fast, and easy. Books self-published through KDP . . . are available for purchase on Kindle devices and Kindle apps for iPad, iPhone, iPod touch, PC, Mac, BlackBerry, and Android-based devices."

Where does KDP distribute e-books to? Also from their Web site: "Your published content will appear on the Amazon.com, Amazon.co.uk, Amazon.de, Amazon.fr, Amazon.es, and Amazon.it Kindle Stores; on Kindle devices; and on apps such as Kindle for PC and Kindle for Mobile Devices. Amazon Kindle owners can access the store directly from their device or via the Web."

Royalties? "You can choose between 2 royalty options for each of your Digital Books, the 35% royalty option and the 70% royalty option. . . ."

A great benefit of e-publishing with KDP is that if you p-publish with Amazon's CreateSpace, both versions of your book will be displayed for sale at Amazon, together, hassle-free.

**Smashwords**

Another popular e-publisher is Smashwords, an e-book file-conversion and distribution service (www.Smashwords.com). You can e-publish for free, then Smashwords takes a percentage as their fee. They covert files into multiple e-book formats so that books can be read on the Kindle, NOOK, iPhone, and several other e-book reading devices and tablets, as well as desktop and laptop computers.

Where does Smashwords distribute e-books? From their Web site: "Smashwords distributes your e-book to the Apple iBookstore, Barnes & Noble, Sony Reader Store, Kobo, the Diesel eBook Store, Baker & Taylor's Blio, and Axis 360 (libraries!) and more."

Royalties? "Earn 60% of List Price from Major Ebook Retailers and 85% Net at Smashwords.com."

**Additional Options**

Also, many self-publishing companies that publish paper books also publish the e version. To locate self-publishing companies that publish both versions, simply page through *The Fine Print of Self-Publishing, Everything You Need to Know About the Costs, Contracts & Process of Self-Publishing*, Fourth Edition, by Mark Levine.

Always vet any e-publisher that you're considering, at Predators & Editors (www.Pred-Ed.com), before you sign a contract.

# How to Price Your E-Book

How do you choose a price for your e-book?

First, keep in mind that people who read e-books expect to pay at least 20 percent less for the electronic version than for a paper version. To their way of thinking, they're not paying for paper, ink, and printing costs, after all.

Next, pricing should be based, in part, on the length of the e-book. You wouldn't want to pay the same for a 20-page book as for a 300-

page book, would you? Exactly. So, it should be priced similar to books whose content, audience, and page count are similar to yours.

Use your Competitor Book Research Sheets, and see if any of those books are available in e-format. Match up page counts and their related prices for the e-books.

Due to royalty calculations at Amazon.com, BN.com, and similar retailers, an e-book priced $2.99 to $9.99 will net you the highest royalty percentage.

See your e-book publisher's Web site to learn how they currently calculate royalties.

## Ready to Publish?

Since each e-publisher works in its own unique way, and has its own requirements for formatting (and therefore could be a book of its own, one that would need to be frequently updated to stay abreast of rapidly changing technology), visit their Web site and follow the instructions there to e-publish your manuscript. Or have an editor format your manuscript file for you, to the e-publisher's specifications.

Happy e-publishing!

Part 6

# Market Your Book
# to Explode Your Profits!

# Chapter 23

# Target Your Marketing Efforts: Interview with Marketing Guru Jim Palmer

Now that you've published your book and possibly e-book, it's time to get your books into readers' (your prospects') hands, and begin to explode your profits!

Used wisely, your book will spotlight you as a leader of your industry. Who wants to work with an industry's leader? Everyone. But more importantly, large, high-profile businesses and ultra-affluent consumers do. They want to experience the outstanding results you specified in your book, and they're happy to pay more than most to achieve those results.

However, for those sales to happen, your prospects must first hear that your book exists.

If a well-written and well-targeted book doesn't sell, the reason is that it wasn't sufficiently promoted.

No book magically sells itself.

Yes, a great book will generate great word-of-mouth sales, but thousands of initial sales must first take place.

Then, if you want to continue to sell your book, you must continue to promote it.

No promotion = no book sales. No book sales = no new prospects.

So. You have in your possession fat, juicy bait. Now, let's slide it onto a hook and dangle it where hungry fish can smell it.

In Part 6, we'll explore several effective ways to do exactly that. We'll delve into **self-marketing** ("self" meaning either yourself or a member of your team who performs this work for you):

**Self-Marketing**

- In the Virtual World
  - o  Social Media, Forums, and Blogging
  - o  Pay-Per-Click Ad Campaigns
  - o  Web Sites
- In the Living World
  - o  Book Reviews
  - o  Magazine Articles
  - o  Speaking Events
  - o  Be a Media Resource and Celebrity

Then we'll consider methods of **team marketing**:

**Team Marketing**

- Your Sales Force
- Marketing Services
- Book Publicists

As you develop your marketing plan, you might use a few of the above, or you might use most of them. Keep all of them in mind.

We'll get started in just a moment. Two questions first. 1) Who is your target reader? 2) What was your specific, primary business goal for writing the book?

Yes, this is a quick refresher from what we talked about at the beginning of the book. Consider your target customer and business goal again.

For example, did you write the book for investors, to draw them into your consultation program?

For entrepreneurs, to pull them into your coaching program?

Did you write the book for homeowners, to sell them on your carpet-cleaning service?

Is your book for soon-to-be brides, to draw them into your wedding-coordination service?

For moms, so they will rent your moon bounces, tables, and chairs for children's birthday parties?

Remember who your target prospect is and your specific, primary business goal for the book.

You want to market only to those fish who are ravenously hungry for your particular bait.

And, you want to dangle it precisely where they're biting. . . .

## Interview with Marketing Guru Jim Palmer

"Where *are* the fish biting?" you ask? For the answer, I turned to Jim Palmer, client, colleague, and an international marketing and client-retention master.

Specifically, Jim Palmer is an entrepreneur, multi-published author, speaker, and coach to other entrepreneurs. A marketing and business-building expert and host of Newsletter Guru TV, Jim is known internationally as The Newsletter Guru, the go-to resource for maximizing the profitability of customer relationships.

The following is from a live interview.

**Tammy Barley:** Jim, I've learned more from you than I've learned from anyone else in my career, so you know I'm jazzed to have you with us. Thank you for welcoming the interview!

**Jim Palmer:** Oh it's my pleasure. I'm excited to be here and share some good nuggets with your readers.

**Tammy Barley:** Let's get right to it. You're a successful entrepreneur, and you also coach many other entrepreneurs. One subject you coach your clients on is using social media to grow their businesses.

As an author of four phenomenal books (to date), you're also an expert at using social media to promote your books, and using book promotion to draw prospects into your business pipeline.

How do you recommend my readers use social media to promote their books, and use that book promotion to draw prospects into their businesses?

**Jim Palmer:** Wow, what a great question. You know, I'm glad you asked this question first, because social media is something that I find way too many entrepreneurs and small-business owners are still not harnessing and using as the very, very powerful business-building and marketing tool that it is.

Now, social media, even five years ago, was probably Twitter and Facebook. But when you think of social media today, there are so many platforms, and more springing up every day. To some entrepreneurs, like myself, who tend to be a little on the impatient side, if something new comes along and someone says, oh, you gotta try this, then it's like, oh no, I don't want one more thing to learn and do.

But what's really happening with the power of the Internet is that it's enabling people—whether you're a solo-preneur or whether you have a small business, or even a large business—to really communicate with prospective clients, readers of your books, potential coaching clients, whatever you're doing. Social media gives you the opportunity to really develop and grow relationships.

Somebody asked me a couple of weeks ago, Tammy, why I do so much social media, because I am really big into Facebook, Twitter, I do the Google+, I do Pinterest now, and of course I do weekly videos,

244

and so on. And they said, well, that's a lot of time. And I said, yes it is. And they said, why do you do it? And I said, there's a whole bunch of reasons, but there's only one *real* reason that I ever log into Facebook or anything like that. He said, why? And I said, because it makes me money. It is a marketing tool, and it makes you money.

How does it do that? Well, the number one way that social media is so powerful for people, is that it helps people get to know, like, and trust you. And no matter what business you're in, whether you sell a product or a service, you *have* to have the know-like-trust.

People have to get to know you, know who you are. They have to trust you before they're going to give you even one thin dime of their money for something you sell, product- or service-related.

And you know, a lot of times entrepreneurs will do that through brand building. If you're big enough like Coke or Pepsi, you can build your brand and get people to know something about you. But for small-business owners, we really don't have that kind of time, and we certainly don't have that kind of budget.

So how do you overcome that know, like, and trust?

Well, you've got to get in front of a lot of people. Certainly, writing a book is a phenomenal way to do that. Speaking is a great way to do that. But another great tool is social media. Social media allows people to get to know something about you.

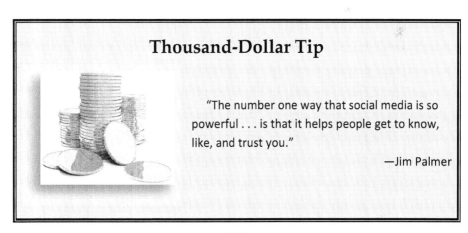

## Thousand-Dollar Tip

"The number one way that social media is so powerful . . . is that it helps people get to know, like, and trust you."

—Jim Palmer

So let me give you a couple of specific ways that social media can help an author promote their books. First of all, if you're on Facebook, you should have a fan page as well as a profile page. If you have a profile page and you started out just connecting with family, things like that, I would start another page.

I use my Facebook, both fan page and profile page, only for business. I do talk a little bit about weekends, kayaking, I obviously talk about my dog, Toby, and things like that, but believe it or not, those are strategic conversations to help people get to know me. But I don't use it as a way to talk to my mother or family members like some people do. I am a business owner, and I'm very strategic in how I use that.

So, a couple of examples. Number one, you obviously want to build some interest in your book, even while it's being written. Tammy, you know that for every book that I've written, I always say, okay, I'm making a commitment, I'm writing my second book, my third book. On the fourth book, I said, it's going to be done in sixty days, that's our goal, mine and coauthor Martin Howey's. So we kind of make a public announcement that the book is being written, and I keep people tuned in along the way, conversationally, through posts on Facebook, Twitter, Google+. I talk about my books and my videos as they're being written.

You're trying to build curiosity. You're trying to build some interest, so when the book does come out, hopefully people are going to be engaged and curious enough to buy it.

Then, when your book is done, you want to create a launch and have kind of a grand opening. Some people actually hire specialists to help you sell a lot of books on Amazon and claim some kind of a best-seller title. So social media is a great way to do that.

So that [information] was kind of pre-book.

The next thing I do is I give the Word document for my books to an editor, and I have them create an enormous pile of blog posts, from little snippets and sections out of the book. Blogging is a very important part of social media.

And one thing that I do when I do a blog post, whether it be about some sort of a marketing or business-building tip—you know, before we jumped on this call, I did one about client retention, which is a lot about what my book *Stick Like Glue* is about—I'll have a blog post about a client-retention strategy, a paragraph or two, and then I actually say at the end of the blog post: "If you want to get more client-retention strategies, check out *Stick Like Glue*," and then I'll put a link to where I sell the book.

I'll then promote the blog post on Facebook and on Twitter. And so you see, it's using all the social media platforms to promote the book. It's all about sharing information and getting people interested.

I'll give you another tip that I use, which is very big for building your client list. About three times a year, I do a Valentine's Day promotion, a Fourth of July promotion, then I usually do a Thanksgiving Day promotion. So three times throughout the year, I will actually give away free digital copies of my books so people can download a PDF copy.

And here's how that works. I will pre-promote it like, hey, next week is Valentine's Day, don't miss my forty-eight hour free book giveaway. I'll do that until Valentine's Day. Then what I'll do is I'll create a special squeeze page or a landing page, a Web site, and it has a picture of me with my book. It might have a sentence—Happy Valentine's Day; I love this time of year, I love being a giver, so I'd like to give you a free copy of my book, but it's only going to be available for forty-eight hours; all you have to do to get a free copy of the book is enter your name and e-mail here, and you'll immediately receive the book as soon as you click Enter.

Now every time I do that, Tammy, I add about three hundred to four hundred people who are connected with me through social media, and therefore I get them on my e-mail distribution list. So that's a pretty powerful strategy.

**Tammy Barley:** So that's how you start drawing those people into your business, through the book promotion and through the book's landing page. You bring those people onto your list, and then you start providing additional valuable information at that point.

**Jim Palmer:** Right. Every one of the social media platforms, like Facebook and Twitter and all those . . . For example, I have 5000 friends on Facebook, which is the limit; I think there's about 10,000 in fans who follow me through the company page; I think there's 32,000 Twitter followers now. I don't for one minute think that there's actually that many people watching my every word, but when I do post something, supposedly a pretty large number of those people will see me.

So I think of this as planting seeds. Whenever I make a post on my blog, whenever I make a post at Facebook or say something on Twitter, I am planting a seed.

If somebody who reads that post likes what I have to say, my number one goal for them is, first of all, to know who I am and learn something about me. But over time, if they like my posts enough, what's going to happen next is they're going to click my name—if they're on Twitter, they'll click my name, they'll read a short bio, or if they're on Facebook they'll see more about me, maybe check out some photos or videos, so they get to *know* more about me.

And if their interest level is still such that says, wow, this guy seems like he knows what he's talking about, or, I could learn more from him, then pretty much on all those pages that I mentioned, there's a link to your Web site. So then they'll go to your Web site.

And the next step there is, every Web site page I have has an opt-in box, with which I offer them some free stuff. The first two chapters of three of my books, and some special reports and videos for their opting onto my list. And that's how you grow your e-mail list.

So you definitely want to try and move people from social media to your list, but also, if that's not happening in a big way, I don't want entrepreneurs to feel down about that, because as long as you're building relationships through the social media platforms, sooner or later, you are going to start getting some new-client business from that.

---

## Thousand-Dollar Tip

"I give the Word document for my books to an editor, and I have them create an enormous pile of blog posts, from little snippets and sections out of the book. . . . I'll then promote the blog posts on Facebook and on Twitter. And so you see, it's using all the social media platforms to promote the book. . . .

"Over time, they're going to click [your] name. . . . So then they'll go to your Web site. [Create a landing page] for building your client list."

—Jim Palmer

---

**Tammy Barley:** I point out in *Business Gold* that a growing number of entrepreneurs are publishing books to spotlight themselves as leading experts in their industries. I also predict that before long, more entrepreneurs will publish a single book for that reason, but the entrepreneurs who publish several books will be seen as the real industry experts.

How has publishing multiple books benefitted your business, compared to when you had only one book in print?

**Jim Palmer:** Wow, what an excellent point, and I hope that's true, by the way—I hope more and more people will publish books. It's something I talk about with my coaching clients a lot. If you want to be perceived as an expert, a go-to authority in your skill set or your field of expertise, there's nothing like publishing a book.

And whether you get a big publisher to publish the book—that's not even really that important. You self-publish your books, and the fact that you are a published author automatically elevates you.

I try and find different ways to help people understand that, because it is phenomenal what being a published author will do for you.

One way that I tell coaching clients this is—because I also promote that you should go out and speak too—I say that when you're a speaker and you're on stage or you're in front of a room, whether there's twenty people or two hundred or two thousand, the very fact that you're up there being the speaker automatically increases your stature and your presence, your authority.

And it's the same way with a book. Once you have a book, you are rising above the others who are, oh, I've got a book in me, or, I'm an expert at this or that. But when you're a published author on that subject, it really takes you to the next level.

So the most powerful thing, I think, is when you're a published author, speak to a group. What I tell people is, you have to really try hard to stink at it for it to have a negative effect, because being a published author in front of a room, speaking to a group of people on the topic that you are a perceived expert at, just elevates you unbelievably.

Writing a book will do that for you.

Writing multiple books is adding more fuel to the fire, if you will. I kind of knew that would happen, but I wasn't prepared for how big the impact would be. As we're doing this interview now, I have four books published. When you have two books, or three or four books, it just adds that much more cachet and prestige to who you are as an entrepreneur. And whether it's real or perceived, you are perceived to be even more successful than you are if you only have one book, or especially if you didn't have any books.

Having said that, Tammy, I did have a strategy when I wrote my books. Five or six years ago, I was best known as The Newsletter

Guru, because I was writing and designing newsletters for companies, which is just a great client-retention tool. And so my first book was called *The Magic of Newsletter Marketing*, and it was all about how to create a great newsletter that will help a business get more repeat and referral business.

That was a natural book for me to write to be my first one. On the cover is a magician's gloves and a magician's hat with newsletters popping out of it, so in other words, newsletters are kind of the star of the book, if you will.

When I wrote my second book, *Stick Like Glue*, that's when I started coaching other entrepreneurs, and I wanted me to be the star of the book, for lack of a better way to say it, and so my name is very big at the top: Jim Palmer, then the name of the book: *Stick Like Glue: How to Create an Everlasting Bond with Your Customers so They Spend More, Stay Longer, and Refer More!*. This book is all about client retention.

So the strategy is twofold. Number one, newsletters are a great tool—I will always be known as The Newsletter Guru—but newsletters are a *client-retention* tool. So my second book, *Stick Like Glue*, expanded on this whole marketing, business-building strategy of *client retention*. In it I talk a lot more about customer service and client-retention strategies. As you know, Tammy, I put my big face right on the cover of the book, and so I sort of became the star of that book, and that helped in a very big way to launch my coaching business.

A year or year and a half after that—as you know, because you edit all my books; you're a phenomenal editor, and I don't know where I would be without you—when I went to launch my third book, *The Fastest Way to Higher Profits*, again, I was on the cover. This is a book that was even one level up from client retention; it's really how to market and grow a business to increase your profits.

I launched this book strategically in September of 2010, and that was a couple of months before I was getting ready to launch a second coaching business. So the fact that I had this third book helped position me as even more successful.

So do you see how that works? I not only wanted to have multiple books, but I strategically wrote them on topics so that each one was going to elevate my reputation. And I also launched them at a time so it was strategic as to when I was promoting my coaching programs.

**Tammy Barley:** So your books really fell into place, to help you build your business. Not just bring in new clients, but new streams of clients.

**Jim Palmer:** Very much so. And I have had some coaching clients tell me—I'm going to boil it down to the way I like to tell other people who are thinking of being an author, so I'm kind of paraphrasing a lot of people—"Jim, my goodness, you do a weekly newsletter, you do weekly videos, you wrote four books, you do this, that, and the other thing. You're the person I want to help coach me because I want to do all that too."

(Laughs.) So, do you see how that works? I'm like, wow, okay. So the fact that I *do* do a lot of things. . . . In fact, I forget where I read this, but somebody was interviewing a very successful business owner, and this owner did a lot of different things, and somebody stood up and said, "Well, it's no wonder why you're successful; look at all the things you do."

I think it was a compliment, but it was almost, "Well sure, anybody can be successful if you do all these different things." So I've always been a person who believed that, yes, if you want people to be drawn to you, and be attracted to you, and if you're looking for people to view you as a mentor, you need to be out there doing things, not just talking about it.

You know, Tammy, you can look at Facebook and Twitter right now and find people who are saying, hey, be an author, you should publish a book, it's one of the greatest things. And then you think,

252

well, *that* person doesn't have a book. (Laughs.) You have to write a book, and you have to write multiple books. You should do video, you should do a lot of different things. But all of these different things that I do are to market and build my business. And it's because I do so many different things that that helps me grow my business.

**Tammy Barley:** Exactly, planting seeds. . . . It's what I call "dangling the bait where your fish are biting."

You know, let me go back to something you said about the Web site that authors lead their potential readers and prospects to. Do you find it worthwhile for entrepreneurs to set up a Web site, or even a Web page, for *each* book? And why or why not?

**Jim Palmer:** Absolutely. You should have a Web page for each book, and a very simple way to do that is, for instance, *Stick Like Glue* is www.StickLikeGlueBook.com. *The Fastest Way to Higher Profits* is www.HigherProfitsBook.com. So to your title, add the word *book* and dot com. Nobody else is going to have that, unless the name of your book is already taken, which is not a good idea. So you definitely want to have a book site.

One of the reasons you want to do that is, first of all, you control it, so you have a good headline, you could do a sub-headline, a big picture of you with the book, maybe you have a bunch of testimonials, or as they call it in your business, praise. So you want to list all the people who have praise because they read pre-publishing copies of your book. So you can list all those things.

If you become a multiple-book author, you'll then have multiple pages for each book, but you also want to have at least one Web site where people can see all of them.

## Thousand-Dollar Tip

"You should have a Web page for each book, and a very simple way to do that is . . . to your title, add the word *book* and dot com."

—Jim Palmer

In my case, I self-publish through my publishing company. It's called Success Advantage Publishing. So if you went to www.SuccessAdvantagePublishing.com, you would see all of my different books there on one page, with the descriptions. And if there's one book that kind of grabs your attention, and the link says Click Here to Read More, when they click there—for instance, if somebody read the paragraph about *Stick Like Glue*, and they wanted to read more, when they click the Read More link, it would take them to StickLikeGlueBook.com, and then they could buy that.

The flipside of that is you also want to be promoting your books on Amazon. You want to set it up so you can sell print copies, and you also want to be selling digital Kindle versions of the book, so you want to make sure you set up both.

Just a little technical tip for the people who are reading this: You have to set those up separately. Amazon runs them almost like two different companies, but there is a way (and sometimes you need to contact their customer-support arm to make sure) that when somebody finds your book, they'll see that it's available—there's a little white box that shows up next to the picture that says paperback price and Kindle price. You actually need to have that created for you.

And another tip for your authors is, Amazon will let you create an author's page. Now, they didn't let me do that—I don't know whether it was because I sold X number of books or whether I had multiple books, or maybe they didn't have it when my first book came out—but when I launched *The Fastest Way to Higher Profits*, they said, hey, you should have an author's page. And I went and filled it out. It's very much like a profile page. There's your picture, your bio. They actually let me have my blog feed, through an RSS feed; when I post my blog, it posts there.

So if somebody is searching Amazon, and they look at my book, if they click my name, my author's page will come up, and they'll read about me, they'll read about my companies. And also on a little column on the right-hand side, in streaming fashion, they'll read my blog posts, so that's pretty cool.

**Tammy Barley:** Great tip. Yes, definitely set up an author's page at Amazon. And, Jim, that brings up a new question. You mentioned that you publish under the name Success Advantage Publishing, and you also mentioned that you self-publish through Amazon, which is CreateSpace. Did you start your own publishing company, complete with legalese, to publish your books?

**Jim Palmer:** No, it's just a different division of my corporation. I didn't actually form a corporation [to become a publisher].

It's actually quite easy. First of all, I think every entrepreneur, for the most part, should at least have an LLC, or something similar, just to protect your assets (I am not a lawyer, I am not offering advice), but I think whenever you are a coach or running any kind of business, you want to protect your personal assets.

And so having said that, I do have a corporation—my corporation is Custom Newsletters, Inc.—and it owns No Hassle Newsletters, No Hassle Social Media, Success Advantage Publishing, I have a concierge print business, and they all fall under the corporate umbrella. So, check your local laws, but all many people really need to do is just grab a URL.

Success Advantage Publishing was available, so you buy that through Go Daddy or wherever else you buy your domains, and you set up your Web page. And then you're off and running.

One thing you want to do is promote that everywhere. So Success Advantage Publishing is on the back covers of my books.

I chose that name, by the way, because when I launched my first book, one of my products was a newsletter called *Success Advantage*. That has since morphed into No Hassle Newsletters. I think Success Advantage Publishing is a good name, and it can stand by itself. I didn't want to confuse people, so I just kept up with that.

**Tammy Barley:** You just threw Success Advantage Publishing out there, and now it's one of your divisions.

**Jim Palmer:** Yep. It's really simple. (Laughs.) You know, sometimes when people ask, how does this work? You just do it. You can just come up with the name, and that's what self-publishing is all about. You can just create a fictitious name.

You might want to do a search through, I think Trademark.gov or www.uspto.gov, where you can see if anybody owns that name, you should do that. In some states, there's nothing you really have to do. Just create the name, file a DBA if required, and run with it.

**Tammy Barley:** A special note to readers: For more information, visit www.SBA.gov/content/register-your-fictitious-or-doing-business-dba-name. In your state, you might be required to register your fictitious business name.

To verify that the business name you like is available, check at http://www.uspto.gov/trademarks/index.jsp, and also google "business name search [your state]" and do a little research there. Finally, google "DBA laws [your state]" and see if your state requires you to register your business name. In some states you do, and in some states you don't. I needed to in Illinois. Fortunately, it was easy and only took me a couple of hours.

If you need to register, your county's forms, processes, and fees may differ from, but should be similar to, these from my county:

1. At your County Clerk's Web site, download and fill out a one-page DBA form
2. Have it (your signature) notarized
3. File the notarized form at your County Clerk's office—$5
4. The County Clerk gives you a notification (intent to Do Business As). Take the County Clerk's notification to a local newspaper
5. The local newspaper inserts the notification in their legal notice section for three issues—$85
6. After the legal notice appears in three issues, the local newspaper alerts the County Clerk's office that their public notice requirement has been met
7. The County Clerk's office sends you a certification that you are legally allowed to do business under your DBA name

Now back to our interview.

**Tammy Barley:** Jim, an added benefit to creating a publisher's name under which you self-publish your books is that the books won't look like they were self-published. The books look more reputable from a reader's standpoint.

**Jim Palmer:** And that's a very big point. Whether you're publishing your book or in everything you do in business, you want to look reputable.

You know, I have a business address although I have a home office. You don't necessarily want to have your home address listed there, so go rent a post office box or something, and list that. You want to present yourself as a real business. Whether you operate at your kitchen table or not is irrelevant. You want to promote yourself as a real business. So, pick your own publishing company name, and promote that. That's really all there is to it.

**Tammy Barley:** Jim, you're an expert in maximizing the profitability of customer relationships. That means long-term customer *retention*, and not just continually working to add new customers into your business funnel. How can readers use their second, third, and even fourth books to help ensure that long-term customer retention?

**Jim Palmer:** There's a couple of things you can do. I've always believed that if you want to sell more of your products and services, the first place you should go is to people that have already identified themselves as buyers, and those are your current customers. So if you're going to market your second book, the first thing you want to do is market it to people that have purchased your first book.

The second people that you're going to market to is everybody else that's on your e-mail list or your distribution list, whatever that is. Promote it to the people that know you.

The third way is start promoting it on social media, so anybody who even knows who you are is finding out about your book.

The next thing you want to do is go out there and do either interviews or speaking engagements, or both.

I did a lot of speaking after my first book came out. Right now I tend to do a lot of interviews for radio stations, people who write articles, and things like that. Obviously the benefit there is that you can do that out of the comfort of your own office. But you want to be interviewed, by anyone interviewing other people, and it gives a chance for their audience to get to know you, and they get to know your audience.

The other thing is, we did hit on this a little bit, maybe pull out the major hook in the book and then start writing blog posts and Facebook posts about that, and drive people back to the book's Web site.

I do a weekly newsletter that goes out to thousands and thousands of entrepreneurs, and my lead article usually has something to do with marketing or newsletter marketing. At the bottom of most articles, I'll say *learn more on this topic*, and I show little tiny image of the cover of that book, and that'll drive people back to the Web site. You always want to be promoting. Always, always, always be marketing yourself and your business.

As I said, there is a hierarchy of who you want to go to first, and there never is one silver-bullet strategy. You've got to be doing a lot of different things.

Somebody who built a successful chain of a hundred stores was asked, what's the one thing you can do [to make that happen]? He said, I don't know one thing that's going to build a hundred stores, but I know a hundred things that will bring in customers.

There's a lot of different seeds that you can plant. You never know which ones are going to grow fastest and highest.

**Tammy Barley:** The difference between advertising as a means of drawing prospects, versus *providing information* (such as a book) as a means of drawing prospects?

**Jim Palmer:** I've been marketing a long time, so it's not something I just picked up when I became an author. I've been in marketing for probably almost thirty years.

As I said, you should always be marketing, and you should always be marketing with a plan and a purpose in mind. There's only so much you can do to just post quotes or different things, and people go, well that's nice. But after a while, they're going to get bored with it. So you need to be marketing with a message, and through that message you want to craft your brand or your image.

You know, most people who know me, whether they're clients or not, or just know me, know me as The Newsletter Guru. They know I'm a marketing expert. They also know I like kayaking, and they know I have a dog named Toby, because of social media. But for the most part, I'm always *providing information* through my marketing, which includes social media, e-mail, and direct mail. I'm always providing information that is going to be helpful and beneficial to somebody who's going to read it.

One of the areas that I think a lot of authors and business owners fall short on is they expect a return too quickly. In other words, if I'm going to share some information—you know, here's five good posts over the course of a week—it's just great information, now my phone should ring and you should want to hire me as a coach. It doesn't happen like that.

I've had people that have, after they purchased a book, two years later they have joined one of my programs. One guy who became a coaching client, he heard me speak four years ago. So you never know. You're always planting seeds, you're always marketing, you're always providing value.

I do know, by the way, the gentleman who became a coaching client this year, who heard me speak four years ago, he has followed me on social media, and he's on my e-mail list, so for four years, or three years, he has been receiving a lot of information, a lot of good posts, I've been sharing some good marketing strategies and tips. He has since seen me write three other books, since I was on that first speaking tour.

So you're always building credibility, and you're always providing value. And I think if you give and give and give, eventually you'll be able to get. But you've got to give first, for sure.

**Tammy Barley:** Jim, amazing information. Anything that you would like to add that would benefit readers to know?

**Jim Palmer:** Well, in addition to the books and the social media, if somebody wants to learn some more strategies, there's two ways to do that. I do put out a weekly video, and I do put out a weekly podcast called Stick Like Glue radio—which is another branding and marketing message there. And the best place to learn more about me is to go to www.GetJimPalmer.com.

**Tammy Barley:** Jim, awesome information. Thanks so much for joining us.

**Jim Palmer:** My pleasure!

## About Jim Palmer

Jim Palmer is a marketing and business-building expert and host of the hit weekly Web TV show, Newsletter Guru TV. Jim is also the host of Stick Like Glue Radio, his weekly podcast on smart marketing strategies. He is best known internationally as The Newsletter Guru— the go-to resource for maximizing the profitability of customer relationships.

Jim is the founder of Custom Newsletters, Incorporated, the parent company of:

- No Hassle Newsletters
- No Hassle Social Media
- Concierge Print and Mail on Demand
- Success Advantage Publishing
- Custom Article Generator
- Double My Retention
- The Magnetic Attraction and Retention Training Program

Jim is the acclaimed author of:

- *The Magic of Newsletter Marketing—The Secret to More Profits and Customers for Life*

- *Stick Like Glue—How to Create an Everlasting Bond with Your Customers So They Spend More, Stay Longer, and Refer More!*
- *The Fastest Way to Higher Profits!—19 Immediate Profit-Enhancing Strategies You Can Use Today*
- *It's Okay to Be Scared—But Never Give Up—A Book of Hope and Inspiration for Life and Business*

Jim was also privileged to be a featured expert in *The Ultimate Success Secret, Dream, Inc., ROI Marketing Secrets Revealed, The Barefoot Executive*, and *Boomers in Business.*

Jim Palmer speaks on such topics as newsletter marketing, client retention, how to build a profitable business, and how to achieve success.

## You can contact Jim Palmer at:

www.GetJimPalmer.com

# Chapter 24

# How to Market Your Book in the Virtual World

Jim Palmer just provided several top (and proven!) business-book-marketing strategies. So what more can the ol' golden girl add? Delighted you asked.

## Social Media, Forums, and Blogging

Why market with these tools? Two primary reasons, which Jim Palmer pointed out.

1. Before prospects will eagerly thrust fistfuls of banknotes in your direction, they have to know, like, and trust you . . . *and* the product or service you provide. Social media enables that know-like-trust process to happen.

2. Once prospects know, like, and trust you (and because you provide highly valuable content at social media sites, forums, and your blog), they'll go your Web site (*they'll* seek out *you* and your book), where you can sell your book *and* capture their contact information with a squeeze page, and then keep building that know-like-trust factor.

   Plus you can then tell them through your monthly newsletters or e-mail marketing about what else you do—new products and services that can benefit them that they might not know about. That can result in sales, and then in additional sales.

Those were two primary reasons. Here are a few more.

3. Through **social media** (like Facebook and Twitter), you can connect with people who have interests similar to yours. In a B2B capacity, that can open up opportunities for cross-promotion. That's how I met Brian Feinblum, chief marketing officer and senior vice president of MEDIA CONNECT media relations, who I interview in Chapter 26.

   In a B2C situation, social media = opportunities for networking contacts. Just today, a social-media friend referred another friend of hers to me as a book consultant.

4. Thanks to the ease of displaying your **blog** posts at Facebook, Twitter, and other social media sites, each post multiplies itself . . . and the number of people who see it. Also, your frequently updated, information-rich blog rises higher in search engine rankings, which brings you fresh streams of prospects who you aren't laboring to reach, but who are laboring to reach you and your valuable content. Those phenomenal blog posts (don't waste time writing any other kind) mushroom the know-like-trust factor, which can then lead to fresh sales.

The key is *targeting*. When you connect with people at Facebook and/or Twitter, target them with precision. Time is money. Don't waste any of it.

If you own a luxury vacation spa in the Carolinas, you don't want to connect with coupon-cutters. You want to connect with women executives who need, and can afford, what you offer.

If instead you produce the ultimate coupon organizing system, don't bother connecting with women executives. Few will be looking for what you offer. Connect with those who need what you provide, more than they need the money that the item will cost.

In short—as with your other marketing efforts—market to exclude those who are not your target audience.

When you participate in **forums**, target the groups you join with the same precision. You can find forums to participate in via Yahoo! (www.Groups.Yahoo.com) and Google (www.Groups.Google.com). When you do, remember that nothing makes people run faster than if you chase them. So, no chasing, no selling. Simply provide snippets of valuable information, leave your name, include a link to your Web site, and occasionally mention your book or perhaps a free offering you have available at your Web site (such as a few free chapters of your book or other helpful free information). Let your considerable personality and urbane charm do the rest.

Social media is free, and it delivers the know-like-trust factor that many forms of advertising cannot. (How often do magazine ads compel you to visit the sellers' Web sites?) Yes, social media requires some time investment. Whether that investment is minutes per day or hours per week, it will be time well spent when you target your prospective reader—and customer/client—with precision.

Social media gets your prospects to come to you.

## Pay-Per-Click Ad Campaigns

"For many businesses, advertising is like a slot machine: You put in your money, pull the handle, and see what happens. Sometimes you do well; sometimes you don't. Either way, you don't learn much that will help you predict the results of your next pull. PPC (pay per click) has changed all that for businesses with the patience and discipline to track online metrics. Just as a gumball machine reliably gives you a gumball every time you drop a quarter, PPC can reliably deliver a customer to your Web site for a predictable amount of money."

(Source: Howie Jacobson PhD, *Google AdWords for Dummies*, 2nd Edition (Indianapolis, IN: Wiley Publishing, Inc., 2009).)

Pay per click is not the best choice for everyone. However, it is an excellent choice for thousands of entrepreneurs who are not making use of this brilliant marketing tool.

Pay per click delivers, to your Web doorstep, prospects who already have interest in buying from you. When done right—which is all-important—PPC can drive up your Web site traffic . . . with the *right* traffic.

And, as Howie pointed out, you can track the results through specific metrics. Then you can make keyword changes in real time. As a marketing medium, Google AdWords is quick, inexpensive (again, if done right), and the results are predictable.

So how do you know if PPC would work great for you? If it will, how can you be certain your PPC campaign is "done right"? In *Google AdWords for Dummies*, Howie Jacobson, PhD, teaches you everything you need to know. Actually, he teaches you just about everything there *is* to know.

If you're going to explore launching a PPC campaign for your book, you'll need the most recent copy of *Google AdWords for Dummies*. It's available for free at many public libraries, or through many libraries as a free e-book download.

Another great book—*Ultimate Guide to Google AdWords: How to Access 100 Million People in 10 Minutes* by Perry Marshall and Bryan Todd. It's ultracomprehensive.

Of course, pay per click isn't like buying a bundle of grapes at the grocery. It's not a one-shot deal. Instead, it's like buying a grapevine. You have to tend it for it to produce.

According to Howie, "When you test multiple approaches, one is almost always better than the other. As long as you keep testing properly and paying attention to the results, you can't help but achieve constant incremental (and sometimes enormous) improvement in your profitability."

Pay per click can be a great way to spotlight—and even sell—your book.

Which, in turn, sells *you*.

## Your Web Site—Does It Produce the Results You Need for Your Book and Business?

As you've probably noticed by now, the reason for participating in social media, forums, blogging, and a pay-per-click ad campaign—all virtual marketing—is to **drive targeted prospects to your book's Web site**.

A book stuffed with valuable information that prospects are eager for, and they know is just waiting for them, will compel them to click to your landing page.

So, their need for your book gets them to your landing page.

The point of your landing page (or squeeze page) is 1) to sell your book, and possibly 2) to give away free goodies related to your book and business . . . in order to **build your customer list**.

That means your landing page must wow visitors. It must compel them to stay.

If it doesn't and they click away, writing your book—and all of the social marketing you did—will have been a colossal waste.

Like reeling in a swordfish and having a hole in your net.

Like purchasing a 1955 Mercedes-Benz 300S Roadster, and then loaning it to Thelma and Louise.

How can your Web site compel visitors to stay? By immediately addressing their pain point.

People buy with emotion, then justify it with logic. So connect with their pain point—whatever is causing them pain or stress and thus compelling them to turn to your book's solutions—and do that on an emotional level. That pain-point connection should be your page header—the first words a visitor sees.

To give you a few examples, I found the following compelling headers from Web pages online. Though these aren't Web sites of books (most book Web sites focus on selling copies rather than providing helpful solutions to visitors), these neatly illustrate the point.

For a business that provides massage therapy, the header:
**Getting away from it all is not as far as you might think. . . .**
(The visitors' pain point is the need to feel relaxed.)

For a business that designs custom homes:
**Step across a new threshold**
**to an oasis, a refuge,**
**one that mirrors the essence of you.**
(The visitors' pain point is the long-awaited need
to own the home of their dreams.)

For a business that teaches dogs obedience:
**Need to restore harmony with your hound?**
(The visitors' pain point is the need to be master of the mutt,
despite the mutt's opinion on the matter.)

Those three examples aren't at all the same as "We provide massage therapy," "We obedience-train dogs," which happens when business owners focus on selling their product instead of meeting visitors' needs.

A gripping, easy-to-read header is critical—Web site visitors only give you a few seconds of their time before they decide to stay a little longer or exit.

What's more, visitors don't want to just read. Visitors want to feel involved.

How do you involve them? First, connect with them on an emotional level, by addressing their chief pain point, and then give them something to do, an action they can take to begin resolving their problem.

Here's how.

- Follow your header with the key solutions your book provides, briefly, in a positive and lively way. Then, offer a free download of one or two chapters of your amazing and gorgeous new book—have them enter their e-mail address so that you can add them to your e-mail contact list—or a link they can click to learn more.

  Be sure to post your contact information in case of technical difficulties during the download, or you could risk frustrating (and losing) someone who had been an excellent prospect. Also be sure that the e-mail download is immediate. Provide just enough content to wow them and leave them wanting more. At the end of the downloaded chapter, with a few brief sentences and/or bullet points, remind the reader of the benefits they will gain by reading the rest of the book. Finally, tell readers how they can purchase the entire paper book or electronic version. Include the links.

- Add a related video they can click and watch—one that further details the book's solutions, one that plays testimonials from your other dazzled readers, or one that enables them to know, like, and trust you.

- Offer them a subscription to your monthly newsletter so they can receive new tips and solutions each month, and so you and your business can stay top-of-mind with your customers. Have them enter their e-mail address so that you can add them to your e-mail contact list.

  To learn how to quickly write and produce effective newsletters—you already knew I was going to recommend this, right?—there simply is no equal to Jim Palmer's book *The Magic of Newsletter Marketing: The Secret to More Profits and Customers for Life* (available through Amazon and other places online and at www.NewsletterPublishingMagic.com).

- Also, on the top right side of your Web page, you might opt to include free bonuses that you'll give visitors when they purchase your book, or you could add those farther down the page, right before your order form.

Offer enough complimentary solutions in the form of valuable free extras, and they'll feel like a moron for *not* buying your book or signing up.

Interactive components help visitors to feel involved, and able to begin resolving their pain points.

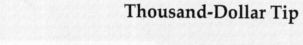

## Thousand-Dollar Tip

Once you have your prospects' contact information, keep in contact. Send them your monthly newsletter. Continue to provide new products and new solutions related to your book and business. Build the know-like-trust factor until they are loyal customers who refer others to you.

It's important to understand that your Web site must include a call to action. Without it, your Web site is just a brochure.

Tell them what to do: Click Here or Order Now. You can either have them purchase the book (and possibly get free goodies) from you, or click through and purchase the book from your self-publishing company. Either way, instill a need for urgency: Now, Today.

Your book's Web site should include key information about you, the author, including the name of your business and the primary solutions your business provides. Keep it short. If you like, you can use your mini bio from the back of your book. Include a link to your business Web site.

Are your header and landing page effective? To be sure, monitor your book site's bounce rate with Google Analytics or a similar tool. If most visitors exit without buying your book or leaving their contact information, you're either not targeting your prospects effectively or your header and landing page are ineffective.

Again, you will need a unique Web site and landing page for each book you publish and promote. Each will be its own pipeline into your business.

Everywhere you promote each of your books, let potential readers know the forms in which it is available: p-book, e-book, a-book (audio, if you choose to produce this medium). If a consumer wants a p-book and assumes your book is only available in electronic format (because they don't quickly see otherwise), you've just lost a book sale and a prospect.

As long as you want to keep selling your book and keep drawing in new customers, you'll need to keep promoting your book. If you want to fill up your bathtub, keep the tap running.

And finally, just as your book's Web site leads visitors to your business Web site, include a Resources or similar page at your business Web site to direct, and link, visitors to your book's Web site. Remember, your being a published author in your specialty elevates you to the position of a leading expert in your field. The more books you author, the more cachet they give.

"Ah, Tammy, great information," you say, "but clearly there's a lot more to it than that. I'm certain the topic of 'marketing on the Internet' alone could fill an entire book."

My dear readers (I answer warmly), my goal with *Business Gold* is to provide you with *every* resource you need to achieve the success you want. So, I will share with you *The Official Get Rich Guide to*

*Information Marketing on the Internet* by Robert Skrob and Bob Regnerus. Not an information-marketer? If not, this book still holds Web site, landing page, and Internet marketing content you truly won't believe you ever survived without.

Chapter 25

# How to Market Your Book in the Living World

## Market Via Book Reviews

Should you consider having your book reviewed by a national book review organization or publication, such as *Kirkus Reviews*? If your book will garner strong national interest, absolutely yes. If your book will be of local interest only, read the following section anyway to help you brainstorm ideas you can use on a local level.

Let me ask you a question. When do you have confidence in going to see a new movie?

I anticipate your answer is along the lines of: When that movie gets "two thumbs way up," five-star ratings by reputable sources, and a lot of excited talk at the water cooler.

Positive book reviews can do for your book what positive movie reviews can do for a new movie—get rated thumbs up by reputable sources. What do those reviews bring about? They give confidence to consumers who then readily step forward with money in hand.

Some book reviews get read by individual consumers. Others by bookstore distributors, and others by public librarians.

There are more than 120,000 public libraries in the United States; that's a lot of potential copies sold which would result in a lot of exposure.

Book reviews can also be syndicated and duplicated in newspapers nationwide, if the subject matter is timely and of broad interest.

Also, you can use positive reviews as testimonials or endorsements on and in the next edition of your book. Remember the gold book cover medallions from Chapter 16: Book-Cover Artistry? A positive review can enable you to put one of those to good use, which will generate even more book sales.

So, having your book reviewed requires only a small investment, and it can generate hundreds of new avenues of promotion, and each of those, in turn, can generate an entire network of enthusiastic responders *who come to you*.

And they won't be the only ones. Since you are now known as an expert, you can be sought after as a resource for newspaper and magazine articles, for radio shows, and for television news interviews related to your field of expertise. That's what happened for Jim Palmer after he became a published author. And that should be one of your goals.

You can add the reviews, and the media exposure they bring about, to your media kit and to future news releases. (Also, add the reviews and information of media interest to your Web sites.)

What's in a media kit (also called a press kit)? Visit www.Advertising.About.com/od/publicrelationsresources/a/presskitsto ols.htm or www.CreateSpace.com/en/community/docs/DOC-1741.

How do you write a news release (also called a press release)? Visit www.GebbieInc.com/howto.htm.

If you receive a book review that isn't positive (grouchy people can turn up anywhere), simply don't use that review. Or, don't use the negative parts of the review.

The following are several top nonfiction book reviewers in the United States:

- ALA *Booklist*—*Booklist* provides book reviews for public libraries, published by the American Library Association.
- *Kirkus Reviews*—They publish a book-review magazine read by bookstore owners/distributors and librarians.
- *Library Journal*—For public librarians.
- *The New York Times Sunday Book Review*—Their reviews are syndicated, and so can appear in newspapers throughout the United States.
- *Publishers Weekly*—Their reviews are read by book wholesalers, bookstore owners/distributors, and librarians.
- A number of other large-distribution newspapers in the United States also do book reviews, such as *Chicago Tribune, Los Angeles Times, San Francisco Chronicle, USA Today,* and *Washington Post.* If you feel one or more of these or your local newspaper's review sections might be a good fit for your book, visit their Web site(s) for more information.
- Special-interest periodicals that match your audience and subject matter might also provide reviews, as well as publish articles specifically for your potential readers.

Currently thousands of magazines are circulated in the United States, and of course thousands more internationally. Target consumer magazines by referencing Writer's Digest's annual *Writer's Market,* available at many public libraries in the nonfiction section.

Quality Books, Inc. is also worth considering. These folks aren't reviewers. They distribute small-press books to libraries, which might or might not work well for your book.

To learn detailed how-to's for all of the above, including media kit and news release how-to's (enough to fill another book), you'll be delighted with *Dan Poynter's Self-Publishing Manual: How to Write,*

*Print, and Sell Your Own Book,* Sixteenth Edition (the red book, copyright 1979 through 2010) by Dan Poynter. Note that his book was intended for people who want to start and run their own publishing company; he turns to book promotion, such as book reviews, in his Chapter 7.

Note that reviews aren't a quick process. Some can take as much as three months or more.

If your book is of national interest, reviews can be worth your weight in gold.

## Market Via Magazine Articles

You're more than an entrepreneur, business owner, or information marketer. You're more than an author.

You're an expert, and a published book proclaims that.

Now, more people need to know you're an expert, so that your business can boom.

How do you get the word out? Write articles for magazines, related to your book and area of expertise. After writing an entire book, article writing should feel similar to writing long blog posts.

In Writer's Digest's annual *Writer's Market*, you'll find magazines that match your subject matter and audience. Some review books, yes, but virtually all publish articles.

After you locate likely magazines, visit those magazines' Web sites to get a feel for their writing style. Their Submissions or Guidelines page will tell you what kinds of articles they're looking for, the word count articles need to be, and who submit your article to.

Write your articles for the same reason you write your blog posts—to provide free, valuable information . . . and to leave readers wanting more, which is your real goal.

Mention your book and business in the article, and include that same information and Web site links in your mini bio that follows the article. Your mini bio should read like the mini bio on the back cover of your book.

Readers will be thrilled with articles packed with great information, and being directed to where they can learn more.

Other benefits of publishing in magazines?

- You don't pay for this "advertising." The publishers pay you.
- Magazine readers see articles as informative and helpful, not as advertising.
- Articles rapidly build the know-like-trust factor.
- Magazine articles give you even more credibility as an author and as an expert—to potential readers/prospects as well as to the media.
- Expanding that thought, articles are an effective way to draw fresh attention to your media kit.
- Writing magazine articles gets prospects to come to you.

Don't have time to write articles? Simply hire and editor or ghostwriter to write and submit them for you.

Feel your celebrity growing?

If not, you're about to.

## Speaking Events

And you thought *Business Gold* was just about writing a book. Mwa-ha-ha! No, my pretties, it's also about how to *Spotlight Your Expertise, Attract a Ton of New Customers, and Explode Your Profits!*

A book is your ticket to the stage. To enthralled crowds white-knuckling their seats to hear every syllable of your next utterance. Crowds who paid to listen to you speak.

Crowds who need your book, and need what your business offers.

It's just, until they heard you speaking on stage, they didn't know what a great person you are. They didn't have an ironclad know-like-trust.

Now that they've met you, the know-like-trust has settled comfortably into place.

Remember what Jim Palmer said: "You have to really try hard to stink at [public speaking] for it to have a negative effect, because being a published author in front of a room, speaking to a group of people on the topic that you are a perceived expert at, just elevates you unbelievably. Writing a book will do that for you."

Here's a bonus hint I picked up from Alexandria Brown, the "E-Zine Queen": At speaking events, if the promoter will permit you, have a free drawing for five or so print copies of your book. You'll collect a jarful of business cards—names and contact information which you can then add to your prospect list.

So speak at several events. Talk about what you know. Provide information of great value. Grow your prospect list.

And leave them wanting more.

Use public speaking to grow your book sales, your business, your celebrity status, and to elevate your media kit to a powerful, attention-grabbing instrument.

Now, that just begs the question: *Why do I want to turn myself into a celebrity?*

## Be a Media Resource and Celebrity

Multifaceted answer: Profit, more business, and the chance to help more folks.

And massage therapy. A custom-designed home. A mutt that obeys. . . .

Whether your book and business appeals at the local or national level, now that you're a celebrated expert, the media—whether radio, newspapers, or television—can seek you out when a news event related to your field arises.

Yes, you might have to publish another book or two, or otherwise get creative, in order to get your permanent star on the media's

Celebrities' Walk of Fame, but you didn't get to where you are by lacking creativity.

So, how do you get the media to find out about you, if they haven't yet? Find and target media contacts, by visiting Gebbie Press (www.GebbieInc.com) or Media Post (www.MediaPost.com).

Next, send your targeted contacts your news release or media kit, whichever works best for your situation.

How do you write a news release (also called a press release)? Visit www.GebbieInc.com/howto.htm.

What's in a media kit (also called a press kit)? Visit www.Advertising.About.com/od/publicrelationsresources/a/presskitsto ols.htm or www.CreateSpace.com/en/community/docs/DOC-1741.

Also, reporters often list the kinds of information they need for articles at HARO (www.HelpAReporter.com). You can connect with reporters there.

Of course, you can also have a representative do all of the above for you, *or* you can work with professionals who provide this experience for you. Details—and an interview!—coming up in the next chapter.

You've noticed that I haven't mentioned placing ads about your book in newspapers or magazines? Trying to sell copies of your book via space advertising is high cost with typically low results. Instead of paid advertising, leverage publicity—book reviews, magazine articles, speaking events, and the media—all targeted to your specific audience.

Not only does media publicity not cost you, many resources pay you, and they result in a better response than an advertisement. Ads are a sales pitch; articles provide valuable, trustworthy information, and reveal a Web site where readers can get more information. Where they can come to you.

So, get talked about, and get your book talked about. Leverage publicity.

Turn yourself into celebrities, my pretties, and your little dog too. There's no place like fame.

# Chapter 26

# How to Promote Your Book through Team Marketing: Interview with Book Publicist Brian Feinblum

Team marketing can be:

- your sales force
- book-marketing services
- book publicists

It's anyone who works with you, or for you, to help promote your book.

*Forbes Magazine* has reported that *96 percent* of business-book authors who sell more than 10,000 copies see a "significant, positive impact" on their business. Those selling more than 20,000? "Off-the-charts" enthusiastic.

This chapter will help you get there.

## Your Sales Force

How can your book be part of your sales forces' marketing effort? Ah, that's just the question you should be asking yourself. How can your sales reps use copies of your p-book, or how might they use copies (or portions) of your e-book?

Here are a few ideas. Your unique business and selling situation may present other creative ways to implement your book.

Give out print books in place of brochures, to affirm your knowledge and experience. They are larger and more memorable than business cards, perceived more valuable than brochures, and will reside in your prospects' offices as a reminder of the solutions your business provides.

Talk about your new book in your monthly newsletters. Include excerpts as helpful tips each month to build your customers' and prospects' interest in buying a copy. Always include a link to the book's Web site where they can learn even more and make the purchase.

Mail a paper copy to every executive, professional, or decision-making problem solver that you want to connect with.

Display copies of your book in your business's sitting area and other customer-contact locations. Doing so can prompt prospect curiosity and give your sales force an opener.

Send out copies to your top clients for your business's anniversary celebration, or give them out as Christmas gifts. Again, they will remain in your clients' offices as a reminder of the solutions your business provides, and help you to stay top-of-mind with them.

Include free copies as gifts whenever your clients make large purchases. Remember, book sales won't make you money; you'll make money because the book sells you.

Few people throw away paper books. They read them, keep them, or share them. What if a customer or prospect shares your book? Then it gets twice the exposure.

## Book-Marketing Services

These folks focus on distribution of your book. They work to get your book reviewed, picked up by libraries, and talked about on the Internet. Many book marketers specialize in certain genres and connecting with certain audiences. If you want to bring in a book-marketing service, be sure to pick one experienced in your subject matter and in contact with your audience. To locate a book-marketing service, visit www.LiteraryMarketPlace.com.

## Book Publicists

Publicists promote you and your book in the media. They, like book marketers, specialize in particular genres, and have established rapport with media contacts related to that genre.

To show you more of what these amazing professionals do, I interviewed one of the best—Brian Feinblum.

## Interview with Book Publicist Brian Feinblum

Brian Feinblum is chief marketing officer and senior vice president of MEDIA CONNECT—formerly Planned Television Arts—a respected, critically acclaimed, and award-winning leader in the media relations placement field since 1962.

In short, the largest and oldest book promotions firm in the United States.

MEDIA CONNECT (www.Media-Connect.com) has promoted thousands of authors and has generated media exposure for the works of best-selling fiction authors Stephen King, Dean Koontz, John Grisham, James Patterson, Nora Roberts, Jackie Collins, Janet Evanovich, and best-selling nonfiction authors Kenneth Blanchard, PhD, Spencer Johnson, MD, Robert T. Kiyosaki, Malcolm Gladwell, Steve Kaplan, Lou Dobbs, Dr. James Dobson, and more.

MEDIA CONNECT has pioneered and continues to be a leader in booking publicity placements in television, print, radio, Internet, road tours, speaking tours, and multiple other venues.

**Tammy Barley:** Brian, it's great to have you with us.

**Brian Feinblum:** It is my pleasure to be here with you.

**Tammy Barley:** Brian, what's the duration and breadth of your expertise in the book promotion field and with MEDIA CONNECT?

**Brian Feinblum:** I have been in the book publishing and PR industry for over two decades, the last thirteen years with MEDIA CONNECT. I have written hundreds and hundreds of press kits and scheduled thousands of media interviews over the years. I love and respect the written word.

I have worn many hats over the years: author, book editor, acquisitions editor, promoter, and marketer. I hold books in high regard and cannot see myself promoting anything or anyone else, except for maybe some nonprofits. Or maybe the New York Mets.

**Tammy Barley:** (Laughs.) Some business-book authors will best achieve their goals with the added experience of a PR firm, while others may achieve theirs by using their current distribution resources—such as their Web sites, social media, blogs, Webinars, seminars, and other established networks—to promote their books. In what situations can a business professional achieve his goals with self-promotion, and when should he bring a PR firm on board?

**Brian Feinblum:** One can always benefit from utilizing a professional publicist. Authors should do what they can on their own, such as blog, Tweet, connect online, build up fan lists, conduct seminars, etc. But in addition to that, they need someone to champion their book and their brand to the news media in a targeted, focused, timely, and effective manner.

Many authors utilize a publicist because they lack the connections, the time, or even the knowledge of how to execute a solid media campaign. I believe it's not a hire or don't hire question; it's really a division of labor question: As the author, what *can* you do for yourself, what do you *want* to do for yourself? As for the publicist, what can he or she do better, in a cost-effective way, that the author cannot—or refuses to—do?

**Tammy Barley: MC Business** is a specialty division of MEDIA CONNECT that, since its inception in the mid-1990s, has boasted several highly successful book campaigns that have assisted business authors to achieve best-seller status. How are MC Business's promotional strategies unique from MC's other service specialties?

**Brian Feinblum:** We love promoting business books. The authors are often looking for publicity that goes beyond promoting the book—or use the book to secure positive media coverage that will benefit them as a CEO, a speaker, a consultant, etc. We offer a comprehensive campaign for business authors and execute at a high level. The campaign usually includes major media: print, radio, TV, and online—and lots of help with media coaching, writing press materials, scheduling speaking engagements, and so on.

We often strategize to help the book become a best-seller or to rise up the Amazon rankings. The business genre, of all genres, is our most successful.

Most importantly, we help further establish their brand.

**Tammy Barley:** At what point of the writing and publishing process should a business professional consult a respected PR firm?

**Brian Feinblum:** I always think it is never too soon to talk to a publicity firm. Often, authors come to publicists at a stage that is late or just barely on time. I think if you can get ahead of the curve with timing, it's an advantage. We can brainstorm and get familiar with the author's background and book. We can strategize and consult with them. We would spend time reading the book and writing the press kit materials way before we contact the media.

We can be a resource early on, as well. In terms of contacting the media, by about four months before the launch date is when we'd begin to contact select print media for advance reviews. For authors who need guidance on their Web site or to schedule speaking events, one would easily start six months prior to pub date.

**Tammy Barley:** What information should a business-book author be prepared to provide when he first contacts you?

**Brian Feinblum:** Here you go: name of the book, summary of what the book is about, author's resume or bio, Web site address, blog address. When is the book coming out or when did it release? Who published/distributed the book? What is it that you are seeking? What are your needs and expectations? What is your track record with promoting a book?

**Tammy Barley:** How do you begin work with a business author to create a marketing campaign for his book? What is the initial process?

**Brian Feinblum:** Certainly every campaign that we execute is tailored to the abilities, needs, and resources of each author. No two campaigns are exactly alike.

We first need to determine the scope of the campaign: What are we hired to do and for how long? Then we set a timeline to execute each step of the campaign. It is important to establish goals and expectations early on.

The campaign begins with us reading the book and developing ideas for the press materials, and brainstorming with the author.

**Tammy Barley:** As a book promoter, in what ways do you work to underscore, or help to clarify, a business author's brand?

**Brian Feinblum:** We do exactly that: help the author determine his or her brand or show them what steps can be taken to support the brand they believe they already own.

To establish a brand, we look at the author's background and credentials—how do we connect the dots? We look at the book's content and other books he has written or plans to write—how are these books related? We look at what the author currently does for a living and ask many questions about where he or she is seeking to go next.

Once we know where he's been and where he wants to go, we map out an approach to maintaining, defining, or expanding the brand.

**Tammy Barley:** Describe the collaborative process that takes place between the author and publicist during the campaign. What is the author's role? The publicist's?

**Brian Feinblum:** The publicist's role is to do what he or she is contracted to do. Of course the publicist can go beyond the letter of a contract, but at the very least, the functions of the publicist should be spelled out in writing ahead of time. We always set expectations and make clear our timeline of planned activities so there are no surprises.

The author needs to work with the publicist as a team, but the division of labor comes down to the publicist contacting the news media, creating press releases, coaching on the media.

The author should supply information, ideas, or resources to help the publicist represent him or her. The author should focus attention on marketing activities: selling the book to groups, looking to set up speaking engagements or bookstore appearances, networking, etc.

**Tammy Barley:** This book's readers are entrepreneurs, information marketers, and other business professionals. Many of them plan to self-publish then use their books to spotlight themselves and their businesses as expert sources for their target customers or clients.

Their book is part of their larger marketing plans, and some authors might not be interested in reaching best-seller status. How do MC Business's strategies complement this layered approach to business marketing?

**Brian Feinblum:** Yes, we do this every day—we understand that business leaders are promoting a book in order to promote themselves and generate business leads and to help them in their branding. For them, the PR will have a huge payoff.

**Tammy Barley:** In your April 24, 2012 blog (www.BookMarketingBuzzBlog.blogspot.com) article, "Measuring the Value of a Book Publicity Campaign," you discuss metrics—how one measures the results of a campaign. How much, average, does a book's success depend on the campaign, and how much depends on the author's involvement and performance in the campaign? Why?

**Brian Feinblum:** Certainly a successful PR campaign involves a collaborative effort between the author, publisher, and publicist. Timing, creativity, skill, and connections, play a key role. You need a great book, and you need luck. So many things go into creating the perfect stew.

**Tammy Barley:** How does MEDIA CONNECT work with authors to ratchet up their audio (radio) and visual (television) performance appeal?

**Brian Feinblum:** We media-train every author. We want them to enjoy the process, to feel comfortable and confident and productive when being interviewed by the media. We know that their performance reflects on our firm's image, so we give it 110 percent to make sure they are ready to have their voices heard.

**Tammy Barley:** Naturally, marketing an e-book will differ from marketing a print book. What are the most successful methods you use to market e-books?

**Brian Feinblum:** Many of the methods are the same: promote a good book written by a credentialed author to the media that likely matches the demographic of your book's reader.

For instance, bloggers and online reviewers or radio shows would be approached regardless of the book's format. But probably an e-book is challenging when dealing with national TV or major print. Most of the major media still wants or expects to see a paper book. That will change, of course.

**Tammy Barley:** Working with a reputable PR firm requires a solid financial investment. How can an author be assured of tangible value beyond the investment of his time and resources?

**Brian Feinblum:** I can only speak about the firm I work for. We bring many years of expertise to the table, as well as media connections and a depth of resources. The client needs to feel comfortable with the firm he or she chooses. The author should ask: Does this firm seem capable? Do they have a track record on my type of book? Who will actually work on my campaign? Do I like the team leader? Does the firm seem to have a passion or feeling for me and my book/topic? Are their references sound?

**Tammy Barley:** The world of publishing has been on a changing course to an unknown destination ever since self-publishing and e-publishing have become contestants in the publishing race. How do you expect book-marketing trends to change over the next five to ten years?

**Brian Feinblum:** I posted some publishing predictions for 2016 recently on my blog: www.BookMarketingBuzzBlog.blogspot.com/ 2012/04/future-of-book-publishing.html. I do think we will see a continuance of more books being published and an increasing portion of them in the self-publishing arena. I think more books will be published as e-only with print-on-demand options available.

I see the bookstore market continuing to contract, and I see that authors and publishers, if they are to find their place in the market or in the media landscape, will have to be vigilant about promoting their books and utilizing outside help to promote their brand and their individual books.

**Tammy Barley:** As we've discussed, many business-book authors will best achieve their goals with the added experience of a PR firm. Every field has its vetted, respected professionals and its bad eggs. How can an author inexperienced with PR firms discriminate between good ones and bad?

**Brian Feinblum:** I would caution authors to get three competitive quotes from publicists. I would urge them to act on referrals from others, where possible.

An author should feel comfortable with the person he or she is dealing with. They should feel the publicist has experience in their genre/field, that the company is established, and that they seem excited to work with the author. You want someone who is passionate to work with you. Testimonials and references are important, but what you need to do is zero in on what the publicist is promising to do and for what price.

**Tammy Barley:** Any other important considerations I haven't thought to ask, that would be of added benefit to the reader or MEDIA CONNECT?

**Brian Feinblum:** I think you would enjoy reading this story that *Publishers Weekly* just wrote about us: http://www.publishersweekly.com/pw/by-topic/industry-news/bea/article/52260-bea-2012-pta-celebrates-gold.html.

**Tammy Barley:** Brian, thank you so much for your time and expertise. We appreciate your knowledge of book promotion and the insider's look into MEDIA CONNECT.

**Brian Feinblum:** Thanks for having me participate. I love to help educate authors and to promote the book industry. If you would like further assistance or guidance, feel free to contact me at BrianF@FinnPartners.com, and do feel free to consult my blog www.BookMarketingBuzzBlog.blogspot.com and our Web site, www.Media-Connect.com.

## About MEDIA CONNECT:
(from their Web site)

MEDIA CONNECT—formerly Planned Television Arts (PTA)— is a respected, critically acclaimed, and award-winning leader in the media relations placement field since 1962. They are a division of Finn Partners, a leading independent PR firm, headquartered in New York, with offices located in major markets throughout the United States.

As a client, you benefit from the respected brand name and extensive resources of Finn Partners, but you also receive close, personal attention under a family-owned business atmosphere with MC.

MEDIA CONNECT provides quality media representation and book publicity to a diverse array of high-profile leaders, including:

- Best-selling authors of every genre
- Leading nonprofit organizations
- Fortune 500 corporations and CEOs
- Hollywood celebrities and pop-culture institutions
- Major trade associations
- The travel and entertainment industries
- Small businesses
- Professional sports figures and popular athletes
- Recognized think tanks and prominent political figures
- Members of the faith community and religious leaders
- Health care professionals
- Members of the news media

**Media Connect Business** is a specialty division that, since its inception in the mid-1990s, boasts a number of very successful book campaigns, including Harvey Mackay's 2010 *NY Times* best seller, *Use Your Head to Get Your Foot in the Door*, and Charlene Li's 2010 *NY Times* best seller, *Open Leadership*. Other recent successes include *USA Today* best seller, *It's a Jungle in There* by Steve Schussler, and George Cloutier's *NY Times* best seller, *Profits Aren't Everything, They're the Only Thing* (HarperCollins).

Other best-seller campaigns include Harvey Mackay's #1 *NY Times* business best seller, *We Got Fired!* and Bill George's *Authentic Leadership*. PTA Business received two BULLDOG REPORTER Media Excellence Awards for its work on Bill George's campaign, including the Silver Award in the General Business category and the

Gold Award in the Personality/Celebrity category. In addition, Media Connect promoted David Silverman's book, *TYPO: The Last American Typesetter or How I Lost 4 Million Dollars* (Soft Skull Press) picked as one of the "Best Business Books of 2007" by *Strategy & Business*.

In addition, Media Connect has conducted Satellite TV Tours, National Public Radio Tours, and Morning Drive Radio Tours for numerous business authors including Noel Tichy, Michael Eisner, Charles Handy, Andy Grove, Michael Lewis, Dave Thomas, Stanley Bing, Harry Beckwith, Stephen Covey, Jim McCann, Jane Bryant Quinn, and Terry Savage, among others.

Media Connect provides many other publicity services and counsel regarding business books, including marketing strategies, media training, bookstore appearances, and special sale opportunities. They also counsel on all Internet marketing matters, Web site development, offer referrals to speaker bureaus, best-seller marketing firms, and bring in various experts to assist them in marketing the book.

They are known for their connections with venues including: Sales & Marketing Executives International (SMEI), Harvard Business School Alumni Club, Young Presidents' Organization (YPO), Entrepreneurs' Organization (EO), American Marketing Association (AMA), Society for Human Resource Management (SHRM), Chambers of Commerce, Business Journals, National Association of Corporate Directors (NACD), International Association of Business Communicators (IABC), and ASTD (American Society for Training & Development). They've also put speakers in front of financial associations such as Chartered Financial Analyst (CFA), National Investor Relations Institute (NIRI), and FPA (Financial Planning Association).

**You can contact MEDIA CONNECT at:**

1110 Second Avenue
New York, New York 10022
Phone: 212.583.2718
BrianF@FinnPartners.com
www.Media-Connect.com

Chapter 27

# One Final Marketing Tool

## An Easy Way to Keep Your Marketing Organized

In his book *Dan Poynter's Self-Publishing Manual*, Sixteenth Edition, Dan has a great idea for keeping track of your promotion and publicity: a simple three-ring binder with five sections.

In the first section, keep your promotional plan in checklist form.

In section two, keep track of expenditures for each edition of your book.

Section three, kudos: testimonials, reviews, and publicity you can use—in ongoing promotion, at your Web sites, and inside the next edition(s) of your book.

In section four, keep your correspondence and important documentation that doesn't fit in the other binder sections. For example, media contacts with whom you have connected or developed rapport. When you publish your next book, that information will be easy to find.

And in section five list ideas for revisions that you can apply to your book's next edition.

Another great idea of Dan's is to keep one copy of your published book for corrections. Label it "Correction Copy" and keep it where you always know where it is. If you find any typos or think of updates or changes you want to make, note them in this copy where the change needs to be. When you publish the next edition, simply make updates from the correction copy.

Whichever marketing plan you create to explode your profits, this simple binder will be a great tool.

## You—the Author, Celebrity, and Customer Magnet

When you started reading this book, you didn't know you'd become all of that so quickly, did you? Yet, you now know *How to Write a Book to Spotlight Your Expertise, Attract a Ton of New Customers, and Explode Your Profits!*

And now that you know all of that, the next book you write will go faster and more smoothly. The next book will also augment your celebrity and customer magnetism. And so will the book after that.

# Bonus!

297

# Competitor Book Research Sheet

**Front Cover**

Book title :

Subtitle (if any):

Edition:

Author(s):

Endorser/Foreword contributor:

Soft or hard cover:

Book cover color/ design/illustrations:

**Back Cover**

Main topics (content) according to the back-cover copy:

Target audience:

Retail price:

**Inside**

Publisher:

Copyright year:

Number of pages:

Attention-grabbing chapter titles:

How my book's audience and/or content will be unique:

# References and Bibliography

## Book Professionals Interviewed for Business Gold:
Ann McIndoo—author's coach: www.SoYouWantToWrite.com
Jim Saurbaugh—cover designer: jsgd@verizon.net
Jim Palmer—marketing expert: www.TheNewsletterGuru.com
Brian Feinblum—book publicist: BrianF@FinnPartners.com, www.Media-Connect.com

## Enthusiastically Recommended Must-Reads:
**If you plan to self-publish:**
Levine, Mark. *The Fine Print of Self-Publishing, Everything You Need to Know About the Costs, Contracts & Process of Self-Publishing*, Fourth Edition. Hillcrest Media Group, Inc., 2011.

**To "develop and implement an effective Internet marketing campaign"** *and* Web site *and* **landing page, all proven to net the most sales with the least effort:**
Skrob, Robert and Regnerus, Bob (with a foreword by Kennedy, Dan). *The Official Get Rich Guide to Information Marketing on the Internet*. Entrepreneur Media, Inc., 2008.

**For unbeatable book-marketing ideas and links:**
Poynter, Dan. *Dan Poynter's Self-Publishing Manual, Volume II: How to Write, Print, and Sell Your Own Book Employing the Latest Technologies and the Newest Techniques*. Para Publishing, 2012.

**To learn how to submit your book to book reviewers:**
Poynter, Dan. *Dan Poynter's Self-Publishing Manual: How to Write, Print, and Sell Your Own Book*, Sixteenth Edition. Para Publishing, 2010.

**To launch a successful pay-per-click ad campaign:**
Jacobson PhD, Howie; McDonald, Joel; and McDonald, Kristie. *Google AdWords™ for Dummies®*, 3rd Edition. John Wiley & Sons, Inc., 2012.

# References and Bibliography

**To implement your client list and grow the know-like-trust factor:**
Palmer, Jim. *The Magic of Newsletter Marketing: The Secret to More Profits and Customers for Life.* Success Advantage Publishing, 2009.

**To rapidly write your book and overcome procrastination:**
McIndoo, Ann. *7 Easy Steps to Write Your Book: How to Get Your Book Out of Your Head and a Manuscript In Your Hands!* 2011.


## Other Bibliographical Resources:
Edwards, Jim and Vitale, Joe. *How to Write and Publish Your Own eBook in as Little as 7 Days.* Morgan • James, 2007.

Glazer, Bill. *The "New" Accelerated A-Z Blueprint Seminar for The Information Marketing Business.* Glazer Kennedy Insider's Circle LLC, 2007.

Kennedy, Dan. *No B.S. Business Success in the New Economy.* Entrepreneur Press, 2010.

Le Blanc, Raymond. *Achieving Objectives Made Easy! Practical Goal-Setting Tools & Proven Time-Management Techniques.* Cranendonck Coaching, 2008.

Palmer, Jim. *Stick Like Glue: How to Create an Everlasting Bond with Your Customers So They Spend More, Stay Longer, and Refer More!* Success Advantage Publishing, 2010.

Palmer, Jim. *The Fastest Way to Higher Profits! 19 Immediate Profit-Enhancing Strategies You Can Use Today.* Success Advantage Publishing, 2011.

Trump, Donald J. and Kiyosaki, Robert T. *Midas Touch.* Plata Publishing, LLC, 2011.

*The Chicago Manual of Style,* 15th edition. University of Chicago Press, 2003.


## Web Sites:
http://www.heasleyandpartners.com/what-is-branding-heasley.html
"What is Branding? Your Answer…At Last."
February 29, 2012 by Kathy Heasley

http://www.millcitypress.net

http://productivewriters.com/2011/02/16/book-e-book-sales-data-united-states-2010/
"2010 Book and E-Book Sales Data for the United States"
February 16, 2011 by John Soares

# References and Bibliography

http://publishers.org/bookstats/distribution/
BookStats Distribution Channels Highlights


http://publishers.org/bookstats/formats/
BookStats Publishing Formats Highlights


http://www.publishers.org/press/68/
"US Publishers See Rapid Sales Growth Worldwide in Print and E-Formats"
May 18, 2012 by Andi Sporkin


http://www.smh.com.au/small-business/managing/blogs/enterprise/7-steps-to-writing-a-good-business-book-20110623-1gg1a.html
*The Sydney Morning Herald* (Australia), "7 Steps to Writing a (Good) Business Book"
June 23, 2011 by Valerie Khoo


http://sunmakers.wordpress.com/2011/05/25/book-myth-i-will-make-money-from-selling-my-book/
"Book myth: I will make money from selling my book"
May 25, 2011 by Ayd Instone


http://sunmakers.wordpress.com/2012/04/04/ebooks/
"Ebooks – the new dimension to publishing and marketing"
April 4, 2012 by Ayd Instone


http://www.time4me.com/theme/write/ebook/3.htm


http://www.writingwhitepapers.com/blog/2008/11/03/10-book-benefits/
"10 Reasons to Write Your Business Book Now"
By Michael Stelzner

# About the Author

Known in the business world as The Millionaire Entrepreneurs' Book Consultant, Tammy Barley has enjoyed a dynamic career for more than a decade, as an award-winning fiction author, biographer, military biographer, publisher, manuscript editor, entrepreneur, and a leading expert in business-book production.

Founder and president of Business Book Productions, she heads a team of hand-picked book-creation professionals, and is also a private editor for entrepreneurs, information marketers, and business consultants in North America.

Tammy has two sons and one daughter in senior high currently writing books of their own, a rescued American Eskimo Dog who doesn't write at all, and thirteen parakeets because the original 'keet needed a little excitement.

www.BusinessGoldTheBook.com
www.BusinessBookProductions.com

If this book helped you, enhanced you, or even dazzled you,
kindly write a review at Amazon or B&N online,
tell others about this book,
and feel free to contact me with your own
testimonial for *Business Gold*
or personal success story with the book you authored, at
www.BusinessBookProductions.com.

Dedicated to your success,

Tammy Barley

The Millionaire Entrepreneurs' Book Consultant

Made in the USA
Lexington, KY
20 April 2013